The MARSH *of* TIME

SAVING SUTTON COMMON

Edited by
ROLY SMITH

HALSGROVE

First published in 2004 by Halsgrove

© 2004 The individual contributors

Front cover illustration: *An artist's impression by* Time Team's *Victor Ambrus of how the entrance to the Sutton Common marsh fort might have looked in the Iron Age.*

Back cover: *Visitors learn about their ancestors at an open day.*

ISBN 1 84114 400 2

British Library Cataloguing-in-Publication-Data
A record for this book is available from the British Library

HALSGROVE
Halsgrove House
Lower Moor Way
Tiverton EX16 6SS
T: 01884 243242
F: 01884 243325
www.halsgrove.com

Printed and bound by D'Auria Industrie Grafiche Spa, Italy

CONTENTS

ACKNOWLEDGEMENTS

WHO HELPED IT HAPPEN

However good a project, however skilled its organisers, without grant-givers and helpers little or nothing could be achieved. All too often they are missed in media reports, or go unseen buried in the small print at the very end, almost as an afterthought, especially when there are a large number. Well here's their accolade, where it is deserved – 'up front'. Thanks to them all.

Land purchase, Sutton Common and Rushy Moor: English Heritage; Heritage Lottery Fund; English Nature; WREN Environmental; Countryside Agency; CCT.
Land management and drainage engineering works: DEFRA Countryside Stewardship; Countryside Agency; Pilgrim Trust; James Goodhart.
Research: Countryside Agency; WREN Environmental; University of Hull. **Excavations** (four phases): English Heritage.

Andrew Booth (Sutton) – farmer; Neil Mitchell (A.P.S. (UK), Beverley, East Yorkshire) – air photographer; Neville Turton, (Everingham) – land management adviser; Richard Watson (Crombie Wilkinson, York) – Solicitor; Mike Husdon (Christie and Proud, Darlington) – Accountant; Grantham Brundell and Farran (Doncaster) – drainage consultants, Dun Drainage Commissioners; Doncaster Naturalists' Society; Doncaster Community Arts (darts); Norton and Campsall Parish Council; Askern Town Council; Askern Miners' Welfare; The Star Inn, Moss; The Doncaster & District Scout Association; Askern Junior, Norton Junior and Campsmount Schools; Doncaster Museum; Bev Weigel – the long-stop on so many things … and the many other local people, students, well-wishers, friends and visitors, who have all taken the project to heart and helped to make a 'Mark in Time' for Sutton Common and the future of the Askern Ward Community.

Special thanks are due to Julia Sheard and the trustees of E. Sheard Family Trust for working out a way to enable CCT to buy Sutton Common – a sanctuary area of the site is named after them – and to Stan Longley for his generosity in freely sharing his historical photographs and research.

DEDICATION

For Jan Knowlson, without whose unswerving background
support this and many other important conservation
projects simply would not have happened.

SUTTON COMMON

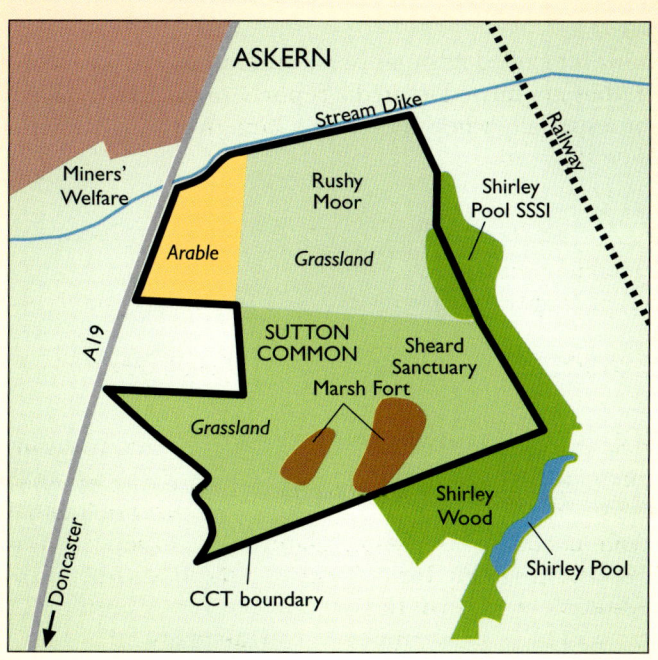

ASKERN

Stream Dike

Railway

Miners'
Welfare

Rushy
Moor

Shirley
Pool SSSI

Arable

Grassland

A19

SUTTON
COMMON

Sheard
Sanctuary

Marsh Fort

Grassland

Shirley
Wood

Doncaster

Shirley Pool

CCT boundary

York

Leeds

Manchester

Doncaster

SUTTON
COMMON

Birmingham

London

York

Selby

Askern

SUTTON
COMMON

Doncaster

FOREWORD

FOR THE COMMON GOOD

By Liz Forgan
Chair, Heritage Lottery Fund

When people get together to care for their heritage, amazing things happen. Suddenly the past starts to galvanise present-day communities, to enrich the places they live in, to rediscover shared identity, to forge powerful partnerships between neighbours and between groups with different interests and experience. At least that's what happens when it all goes right.

Sutton Common is a living example of such a project where many different bodies and agencies have made the most of their individual expertise and skills, working as a team to achieve something much, much more than the sum of its parts.

It has become a national flagship project for archaeological and environmental conservation and for community partnership. The project has successfully linked archaeology, ecology, wildlife and heritage, farming and land management, community and education work. It has not only benefited the former coalfield town of Askern and Sutton Common itself, but also the wider scientific and archaeological community.

The wetland research and science-based landscape conservation carried out here was at the cutting edge of technology, and constituted work of international significance. As a partnership project, it is one of the most successful so far undertaken in the country. That partnership – which reflects the web of inter-relationships within the community and in the environment – has been the key to the project's success.

I commend both the exciting, pioneering work done at Sutton Common and congratulate all those who took part – from the archaeologists and scientists to the schoolchildren of Askern and district.

If any other communities are looking for a way forward but find themselves frustrated by red tape and regulations, hampered by lack of information (or too much of it), or bogged down with many disparate initiatives, they could do well to follow the example set by the Sutton Common project.

INTRODUCTION

A JOINED-UP-JOB

By Ian Carstairs

I know an old lady who swallowed a bird,
How absurd to swallow a bird.
She swallowed the bird to catch the spider,
That wriggled and tiggled and tickled inside her.
She swallowed the spider to catch the fly,
I don't know why she swallowed the fly…

Funny how I should think of that childhood ditty as I savoured Robert Booth's rum-and-raisin ice cream on a scorching Sunday afternoon in the centre of the Iron Age enclosures on Sutton Common.

It was the last open day, and Jan, the then chairman of the Carstairs Countryside Trust, had just asked: "Where did the milk come from for your ice cream?"

"My brother Andrew's cows," Robert replied.

I smiled to myself – and that's what started me thinking …

…the ice-cream was made from the milk, which came from the cows, which ate the grass, that Andrew farmed, which the trustees created, that helped the archaeology and boosted the wildlife, which people could use to improve their town, paid for through taxes and tickets, by people who came… and ate the ice cream, which cooled their thirst, on a scorching afternoon, as the cows grazed on …

…and all because of mysterious events in this extraordinary place more than two thousand years ago.

Do you get the idea? What a wonderful, remarkable joined-up-job *The Marsh of Time* at Sutton Common has become.

But let us take a step back for a moment.

There are many points in history where I could have started this unique story. I could have begun 12,000 years ago as the ice sheets retreated and a great lake

Ellerton Abbey Garth and Ellerton Ings, lying between the church and the river, bottom left.

known as Lake Humber formed over a vast area of Yorkshire and Lincolnshire.

Or about 2,500 years ago in the Iron Age, when those ancient people built curious structures on two islands in the marsh which fringed where the lake once lay.

Instead, I have chosen to begin in spring 1989 on a flyover where the Hull Road crosses the York by-pass. It was here that the Carstairs Countryside Trust (CCT), which would spearhead the remarkable story of co-operation at Sutton Common, was born.

I had just received a generous gift of a sum of money, presented as a token of appreciation for a major conservation project I had run. As I turned onto the flyover, it came to me that it might be a good idea to use the money to set up a charity. This was the time of high interest rates and I fondly imagined the trustees sitting down each December to give away the interest to conservation causes which took our fancy.

But it didn't quite work out like that.

No sooner had CCT come into existence than English Nature encouraged us to buy an important hay-meadow at Ellerton Ings in the Lower Derwent Valley. The land also included Ellerton Abbey Garth, the site of a twelfth century Gilbertine priory. We accepted the challenge, put in an offer and within a few months found ourselves embarking on a journey of fund-raising land ownership and management.

Shortly after taking possession, we discovered the neighbouring church was set to be demolished. We were despondent: it had been the magnificent setting of the church overlooking the Abbey Garth which had in part inspired us to buy the land in the first place. However, it soon became clear that since we now

Ellerton Church.

owned the surrounding land we could grant a new access to the church – the cause of one of its problems – which would enable the future to be secured.

It was disturbing to think that this beautiful landmark was on the verge of demolition when the church authorities agreed to transfer it to a new trust, the Ellerton Church Preservation Trust, which had been specifically formed to save it.

It was during negotiations over the future of the church that we first heard about Sutton Common. Sitting in the St Vincent Arms in Sutton-upon-Derwent, Jon Etté, English Heritage's Inspector of Ancient Monuments put his head in his hands – explaining he had just come from the "most terrible and intractable problem." It was, he said, one of the most important Iron Age sites in the country, yet it was drying out and soon all would be lost with no-one ever knowing what it had all been about.

The trustees looked silently at each other; each knew what the others were thinking.

Sutton Common, showing the small enclosure, under arable cultivation.

"We'll try to get it," I said to Jon, "but we'll need some help."

Having said we'd have a go, we actually didn't know where Sutton Common was. In fact, we never saw it for some two years until most of the negotiations to acquire it were complete.

Buying land with grant-aid is never easy. Luckily, the owners, the Sheard Family Trust, were very sympathetic, but they faced a major problem: the land was locked in a three-generation agricultural tenancy .

At a meeting in the Great Northern Hotel, King's Cross, Julia Sheard, one of the owners, explained she was willing to try to negotiate an arrangement with the tenant, such that a sale might be possible, but warned it could be a slow process. So, a basic plan was agreed. In parallel, for our part, we set about raising the money. At a price of approaching £150,000, there are only a few place from which a small charity can attract this level of funds – from Government bodies and the Heritage Lottery Fund. But that was by no means an easy call.

Normally you need to show how the land will be managed and how public access will be provided before a grant is made. We simply didn't have the answers to those questions, knew we never would unless the land was in our ownership, and at this stage, we certainly couldn't have consulted the community in such a delicate situation. To our good fortune, both organizations agreed that acquisition was 'simply everything' and once under the Trust's control the wider work to preserve the site and provide access could be agreed. The scene was set and after three years the sale went through.

Soon after the Trust bought Sutton Common, June Jordan and Peter Darvill from Norton and Campsall Parish Council wrote to us asking if we would include them in our work. It was the local head-start we had hoped for, and we met the council for afternoon tea, rather than attend their formal public parish council meeting.

An enormous amount of work lay ahead, particularly as we also had our eye on another area of land known as Rushy Moor, which lay between Sutton Common and the outskirts of Askern. We shared our ideas with the councillors, asking them to keep a confidence and after a further two, sometimes nail-biting years, Rushy Moor was under the Trust's control too, and we were ready to go public.

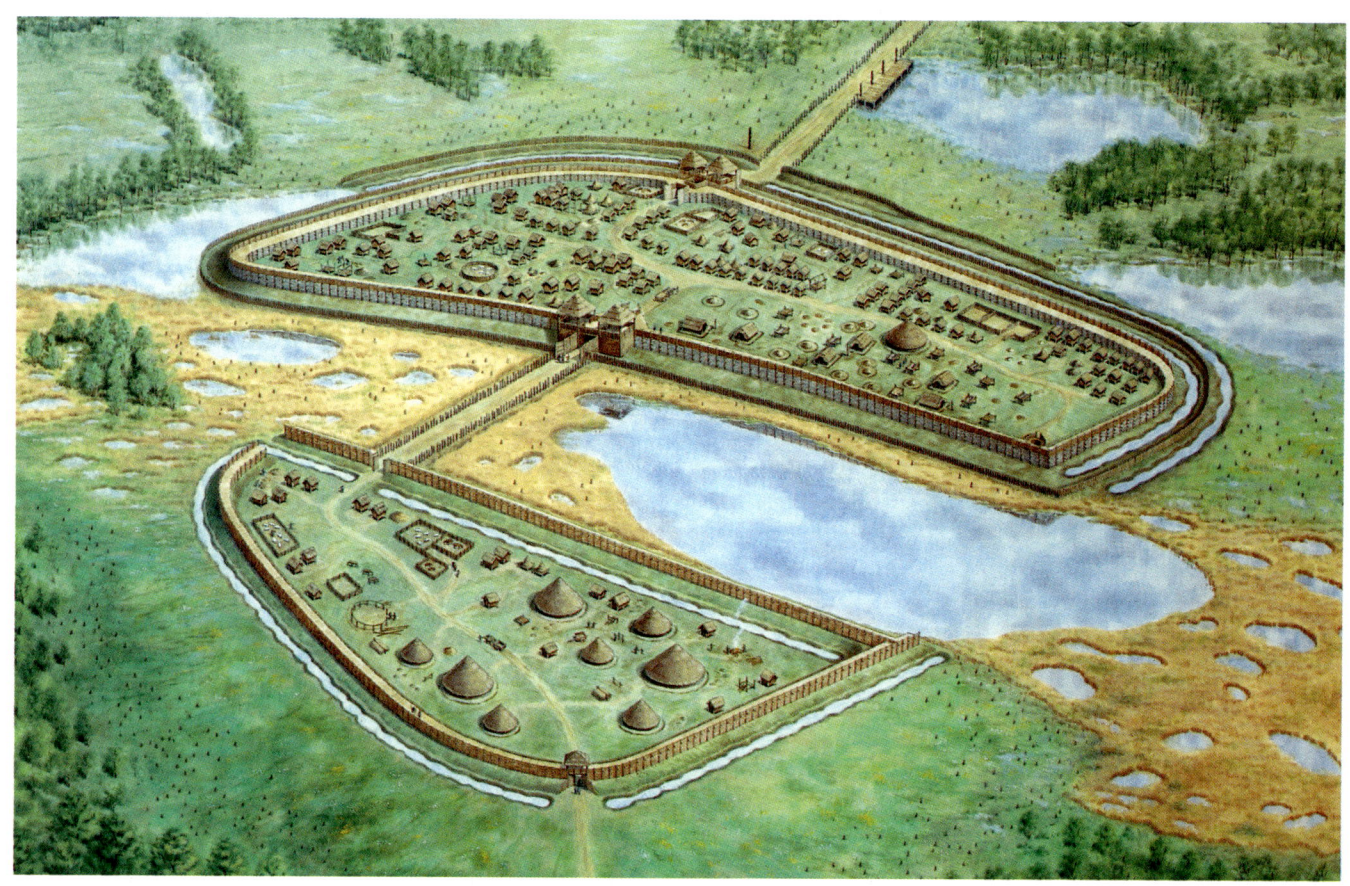

Based in part on the results of excavations, this artist's impression shows how the Sutton Common site might have looked if it had been completed and occupied. No evidence has yet been found that houses were ever constructed.

THE SUTTON COMMON PROJECT

The Sutton Common Project, which includes land acquisitions, wildlife and landscape enhancement, archaeological and palaeoenvironmental evaluations, research and conservation, and engineering works to raise groundwater levels, is spearheaded by the owners of the land, the Carstairs Countryside Trust (CCT), in partnership with English Heritage, English Nature, Countryside Agency, the Universities of Exeter and Hull and Grantham Brundell and Farran.

The Project forms one of the Countryside Agency's trial schemes in the Humberhead Levels 'Value in Wetness' Land Management Initiative, which is seeking new, economically viable and environmentally sustainable approaches to water and land management in the Humberhead Levels.

Close collaboration with the North Doncaster Rural Trust over future public access and enjoyment of the site seeks to contribute to the environmental and economic regeneration of Askern Ward in this 'Coalfields' area of South Yorkshire.

The Sutton Group, lead by Henry Chapman, strung out in a line across the route of the causeway in 2000.

Once the site had been acquired, an ambitious vision was set out for management and conservation of the whole landholding and how it might link to the town. This included direct conservation of the archaeological remains, improvements for nature conservation and securing the future of the Shirley Pool Site of Special Scientific Interest which lay alongside the Common, as well as the all-important tie-ups with the Askern Ward community.

An informal Sutton Common Group embracing a wide range of interests evolved to steer the work. It was never set up, it just happened and grew. Having worked extensively with Government bodies, local authorities and charities, and knowing the minefield this can sometimes become, we were determined that the emphasis would be on action, not on words and paper. From the outset the Group, spearheaded by CCT trustees, held meetings only when they were absolutely necessary, without minutes or complex agendas and with guidance for the whole project stemming from a simple two-side A4 vision and one map. Over the last seventy years many small-scale archaeological investigations of the enclosures have been undertaken, but they were of little help with our main issues. It was vitally important to assess the condition of the buried deposits, then judge to what extent it would be possible to reverse the drying-out caused by local drainage schemes.

These schemes had been undertaken to counter the effects of mining subsidence and to improve agricultural production, and had lowered the groundwater levels by more than a metre in twenty years, causing the buried archaeology to deteriorate. Organic materials – wood, pollen and plant and animal remains – which had lain preserved in the oxygen-free, wet conditions for two and a half thousand years, were degenerating rapidly, virtually before our eyes.

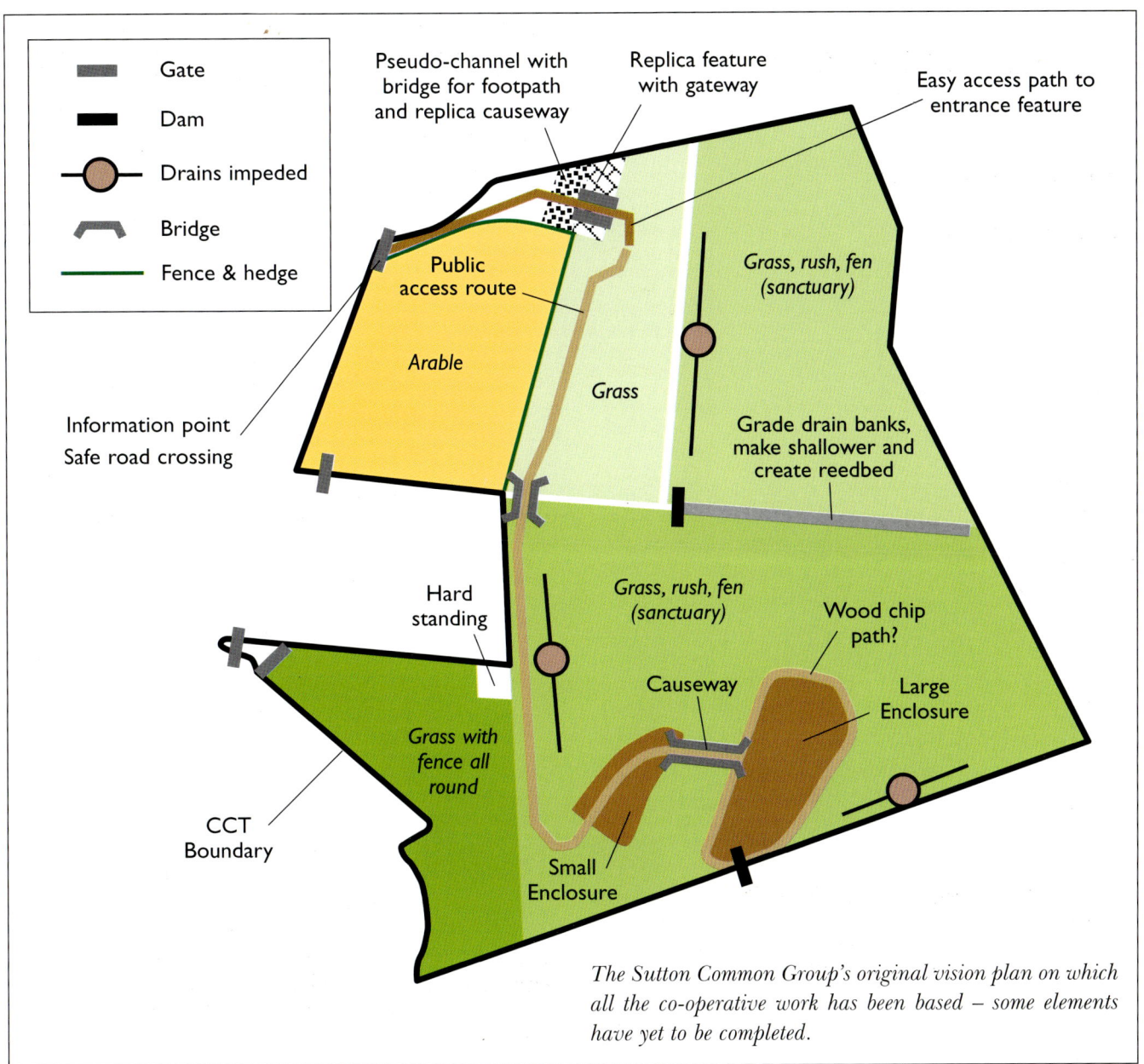

Legend:
- Gate
- Dam
- Drains impeded
- Bridge
- Fence & hedge

Pseudo-channel with bridge for footpath and replica causeway

Replica feature with gateway

Easy access path to entrance feature

Information point
Safe road crossing

Public access route

Arable

Grass

Grass, rush, fen (sanctuary)

Grade drain banks, make shallower and create reedbed

Hard standing

Grass, rush, fen (sanctuary)

Wood chip path?

Causeway

Large Enclosure

Grass with fence all round

CCT Boundary

Small Enclosure

The Sutton Common Group's original vision plan on which all the co-operative work has been based – some elements have yet to be completed.

Since its first land acquisition in 1989 – the Trust now manages some twenty sites – CCT has used air photography, provided by Neil Mitchell, as an essential tool to support its work. Although based many miles away in Beverley, Neil used a farm aerodrome close to Askern. He was therefore able, quite inexpensively, to cover the Common virtually whenever we wanted it done.

As the seasons and vegetation changed, Neil's photographs proved an invaluable resource, not only for depicting the archaeological remains and excavations, but also for revealing the braided prehistoric river channel of the Hampole Beck within which the enclosures lay and at the same time showing whatever was going on in the surrounding landscape.

Before trying to raise the water table, the trustees firstly needed a detailed levels survey as well as an accurate understanding of the existing water table and how it fluctuated throughout the seasons.

Thus, the intensive research at Sutton Common began with a new detailed survey by Henry Chapman. The data acquired would reveal the micro changes – down to 1cm accuracy – in the surface and also enable us to relate them precisely to groundwater levels. These were assessed using piezometers – essentially plastic tubes sunk into the ground – down which measurements to the groundwater level can be taken.

The trustees also needed to decide how the land would be managed. Luck was on our side here too. A neighbouring farmer, Andrew Booth, whose family had known the common before it had been ploughed, was keen to farm the land. We had agreed with the grant givers that eight hectares of arable land would be farmed commercially as a working endow-

ment to help support the maintenance of the associated conservation grasslands. We were also successful in gaining a Countryside Stewardship agreement, which helped immensely by providing funding to support the complex activity which would follow.

Andrew Booth, farmer.

Put bluntly, to begin with the whole 55-hectare site looked a disastrous mess. After a number of years in set-aside, one could be forgiven for wondering whether a grassland could ever be recreated. Yet within three years, by judicious mowing and some fierce thistle-controlling, Andrew turned the site round to the point where it was almost unrecognisable in comparison with the tangle just a year or two earlier.

It was interesting to watch the vegetation change. Initially, vast mats of rush spread across the fields, then, once the rushes had been cut, thistles nearly two metres high blanketed the scene: there was simply no option but to spray them.

With reversion to grassland underway, fences erected, hay crops taken and cattle grazing, we turned our attention in earnest to the groundwater levels and the conditions of the buried organic archaeological remains. There were a number of questions to be answered depending on the condition of the remains: could any be preserved *in situ*; what would be lost within our lifetime; what was on the borderline for survival, and what were their positions in the strata in relation to the groundwater?

We also needed to know the raised groundwater levels required to stand a chance of re-creating the still wet conditions needed for preservation. From this detailed information we could plan the engineering works to deliver the maximum possible increase in water levels without flooding adjacent land.

To introduce our proposals, I addressed a meeting of the Dun Drainage Commissioners. As the Internal Drainage Board for the area, the Commissioners would have to approve any scheme for changing the drainage patterns and raising water levels. To identify the necessary works we then commissioned Grantham Brundell and Farran, Consulting Drainage Engineers. Their brief was relatively straightforward: "Investigate the works necessary to raise the water table and keep the water on the site."

David Patrick from GBF co-ordinated the research and tested the feasibility of our requirements. His solution involved, not as one might think, the destruction of the field under-drains, but re-engineering the pipes near their outfalls to control the height of the groundwater on the Common, while leaving the final outfall into the ditches at the same level.

Once in place, the works had an immediate effect, but while we had stopped the loss in one direction, the water was now running out in the other direction through Shirley Pool. Dams were needed in two lateral drains. They were soon installed and further helped stem the flow of water from the site.

With engineering works completed, a programme to monitor their impact had to be devised. In the early stages of data gathering, James Cheetham, a student at the University of Hull, monitored water levels on the Common. Fortunately, CCT, with the support of the Countryside Agency and WREN Environmental, was then able to sponsor James on a three-year PhD research project as part of the Humberhead Levels Value in Wetness initiative to evaluate the success and effect of the engineering works.

There were other elements to the research too. Aerial photographs were taken every month to monitor wetness and vegetation change and, using the Trust's land agent Neville Turton, an economic appraisal was undertaken to compare the potential income as an arable enterprise with that of managing it for wet grassland under a Countryside Stewardship agreement, with the aim of helping others interested in similar schemes.

James devised a series of experiments at the very cutting edge of scientific understanding to measure the effects of re-wetting an archaeological site. Through his analysis we hoped to determine whether or not the re-wetting had successfully arrested the deterioration of buried organic remains.

Scientific research provided one area of contact for the project with the educational world. Another grew out of our work with local schools. Ian Panter, the Regional Scientific Adviser for English Heritage, developed an idea where students worked on a 'Rubbish and Archaeology project.' Left-overs of lunches were buried in both wet and dry environments to be dug up a year later. From the smelly remains recovered it was clear that different things did happen, demonstrating directly to students the principles which have led to the survival of organic material in the wet common for thousands of years.

Obviously, the most exciting parts of the project have been the excavations to find out what happened at Sutton Common in the past.

Robert Van de Noort, Jon Etté and James Cheetham at a trial trench at the centre of the causeway.

Firstly we needed to discover what, if anything, remained in the large enclosure. Having been bulldozed in 1980 it was generally thought that anything which did exist had been destroyed and that the centre of the enclosure never contained anything anyway. But Robert Van de Noort, director of the excavations, orginally from the University of Hull and now with the University of Exeter, thought differently. His prophetic words still stick firmly in my mind as one the defining statements of the whole scheme. "Look, I have driven a bulldozer and you simply cannot move that amount of earth to destroy the entire site without there being a big pile somewhere else. The banks were simply pushed into the ditches, so the centre and ditches of the large enclosure will still be there," he said. He would be proved absolutely right.

The first phase involved four trial trenches. These limited works revealed, not only the entrance way to the large enclosure, but also clear evidence that the two enclosures had been linked by a causeway. The work also enabled us to judge the state and depth of preservation of the prehistoric wooden posts, which would help set the target for increased levels of groundwater, as well as inform the plans for any future excavations.

There were to be three more annual phases of major excavations, all focused on the large enclosure, where it had become abundantly clear that the remains were in such a poor and deteriorating state that they would not survive our lifetimes, or even perhaps a few more years. And if this work was not done now, the opportunity to look through an open window into the lives of people in the Iron Age would be lost.

The next stage involved removing the ploughsoil over the whole entrance to the large enclosure as

From left, Mike Corfield, Robert Van de Noort, David Miles and Jon Etté discuss the opportunities for major excavations.

well as opening up sample strip-trenches across the area. The results were extremely encouraging. Alignments of wooden posts, the foundations of a limestone wall and a well were clearly visible. Most importantly, the trial trenches proved conclusively that there had been structures within the large enclosure as Robert has predicted – it certainly was not completely empty!

There was however a puzzle; other than a part of a bronze bangle and one flint arrowhead, no artefacts had been found. By now, speculation in the media ran way ahead of the facts, describing the causeway and entrance in bold and grim headlines as a "Gateway to Death," based on an assumption by journalists that this would have been a one-way road to the bog beyond for those about to be sacrificed. Not a shred of evidence existed to support such a statement.

Following a visit by English Heritage's Chief Archaeologist, David Miles, their Chief Science Adviser, Mike Corfield, Jon Etté and new Ancient

Monuments Inspector for the area, Keith Miller, a major excavation campaign was planned. This aimed to remove almost the whole of the ground surface of the large enclosure. The task would be undertaken over two years, with four huge 100m x 30m trenches, 30 metres apart being opened-up in year one, and the alternate strips in year two. This would be one of the largest excavations of its kind ever undertaken on a wetland site.

When work began in earnest in late June 2002, with soil clawed away carefully by a huge mechanical digger, expectations ran high. And we were not to be disappointed: just 400mm below the surface of the field, lay evidence of a complex range of structures. Thousand of post holes, many still containing the remains of 2500-year-old wood, dotted the creamy-coloured sub-soil.

But despite all the evidence, no clear signs as to what the structures were and exactly what people were doing here was found. In fact, there remained a fundamental mystery – there was no sign that people had ever actually used the place at all. A further rush of newspaper headlines now heralded the: "Discovery of Yorkshire's Ghost Village."

A year later at the start of the final phase of excavations and with an opportunity to reflect on the analysis of material found the previous years, ideas emerged that the site might have been a huge grain store, which had failed for some unknown reason.

By now, the term marsh-fort – a sort of hill-fort in the lowlands – had been coined to describe the site, but unlike its upland counterparts where no evidence of the wooden structures and human habitation remain, here the wet boggy conditions had preserved a wide range of evidence.

Everyone involved with the project had always been cautious about publicity for fear of attracting unwelcome attention to the excavations. Near the end of the dig, reports came in that a skull had been found set in the ditch beside the eastern entrance.

Robert called the police, who having established that the person was more than 500 years old, lost interest in the skull but became fascinated by the dig and the archaeological detective work being carried out here. What we hadn't reckoned on, however, was that the police would mention their attendance to the press. I suppose it brightened up what otherwise might have been a quiet news day. Within twenty minutes local newspapers were on the phone wanting to know about the finds.

The police were also involved in another rather comical event as we prepared for the final open day, which had been so admirably developed by Helen Fenwick of Hull University. Arrangements had been made for cones and signs to be used on the main A19 road, to warn motorists of the awkward entrance. Late in the preceding afternoon, the community policeman called my mobile. He apologized profusely explaining that the insurance companies had stipulated that the police were no longer able to provide safety cones and signs in case a member of the public tripped over one and sued! We agreed, it was another collectors-piece example of the death of common sense.

The sun, so they say, shines on the righteous. By that token, when it comes to public open days, we must be right up there in the stratosphere, as each of the annual open days were blessed with perfect weather. With brilliant, sunny days, two blisteringly hot, there was a beach-like, carnival atmosphere as large numbers turned out to engage with the world of their ancestors.

James Cheetham enthrals visitors to a Sutton Common Open Day.

What impressed us all about the visitors was the extent of their knowledge and sophisticated understanding of quite subtle features, often no more than grey smudgy manifestations in the soil where long-gone structures once stood. For this, I have no doubt, popular television archaeology programmes must take the credit. And the word 'geophys' rolled off the tongue as though it were everyday language.

I especially recall a couple bespangled with rings and tattoos and grasping tightly their copy of *Current Archaeology* walking across the difficult terrain in the ancient river channel between the enclosures, pushing a full-size pram and trailing an impressive rotweiler.

As I approached, they enquired who had paid for everything?

"Many organisations, but English Heritage paid for the excavations and the Heritage Lottery Fund put in a lot of money too," I replied.

"You mean lottery money goes into things like this?" they continued.

"Yes," I said, rather hesitantly, awaiting the next comment.

"Well if that's the case, we'll keep doing the lottery," they stated emphatically.

With between 500 and 1000 visitors to each open day, it all felt wonderfully worthwhile. But for me the best bits were right at the end.

One involved John Riddle, a member of the shooting syndicate we allow to cross our land to enter the neighbouring wood. "I've got something I'd like to present to you," he said, passing his camera to his wife Barbara to take a picture. From his pocket he produced a large, beautiful Neolithic flint axe-head. "Someone found it over there on the ditch-side while they were walking to the wood. It's taken me months

John Riddle (right) *presents Ian Carstairs with a Neolithic axe-head found by a ditch.*

to get it back. It belongs with you," he explained proudly and thrust it into my hand.

I was greatly impressed by the effort John had gone to over something about which we would have been none the wiser. I handed it back to him. "Take it to Henry, he looks after these things – he's on *Time Team* on the television, and I'll take your photo presenting it to him." John beamed from ear to ear.

I have often been asked: "How did you all manage to make it work and to do it without any bureaucracy?" The answer is actually very easy: a clear idea, strong sense of direction, mutual respect, confidence between everyone who has played a part and personal commitments to the project by everyone involved, no matter who you represent.

This book is effectively a permanent record of some of the team's presentations at our Sutton Common conference *Time Present and Time Past* held in the summer of 2003, as well as also recording the efforts of many others who also played vital but unseen parts. But if one person should be picked out for special mention, it is Jon Etté, who compromised his weekends and evenings over several years and never once complained about the many times I depended on his advice and guidance to move quickly through the labyrinth of decisions which needed to be made just to get us to the starting gate. He never failed us once.

Time Present and Time Past – a conference held by the Sutton Common Group in Askern Miners' Welfare.

IAN CARSTAIRS

Ian qualified as a graphic designer and photographer and is a countryside conservation project consultant, working principally with statutory bodies, local authorities and charities. He is chairman of the Heritage Lottery Fund's Yorkshire and the Humber Regional Committee and of the Light Owler Trust; a member of the Forestry Commission's Yorkshire and the Humber Regional Advisory Committee, and a trustee of York City Charities. He was appointed an MBE in 1995 for services to conservation. He founded CCT in 1989 and co-odinates the Sutton Common Project.

CHAPTER ONE
AFTER THE ICE

MALCOLM LILLIE starts the story of Sutton Common and the landscape of the Humberhead Levels from the end of the last Ice Age, when it was under the waters of the former Lake Humber, to its use by farming communities in the Bronze and Iron Ages.

The image which perfectly encapsulates the long history of Sutton Common is the electricity pylons striding across the landscape. It shows the span of several thousand years in one picture, for the pylons stand on sandhills left after the ice sheets retreated, and where the earliest traces of human activity have been found on the Common.

Before embarking on an account of the land and people in late prehistoric times, it is useful to outline the landscape processes at work in the region from the end of the Ice Age.

Our story starts in the late-glacial period (18,000-10,200 years ago) when the retreating ice sheet lay to the north of the Humberhead Levels, and meltwater formed an extensive ice-dammed lake known to archaeologists as Lake Humber. The lake itself is unlikely to have been a single vast expanse of water, but was probably interspersed with 'islands' of sands and gravels deposited by the ice. Eventually the lake filled in with sediment, forming a plain which, along with the sands and gravels, forms the upper surface of geological deposits which cover this lowland region. It was at this time that the forerunners of the rivers of

Two electricity supply pylons stand on former islands within the prehistoric marsh.

21

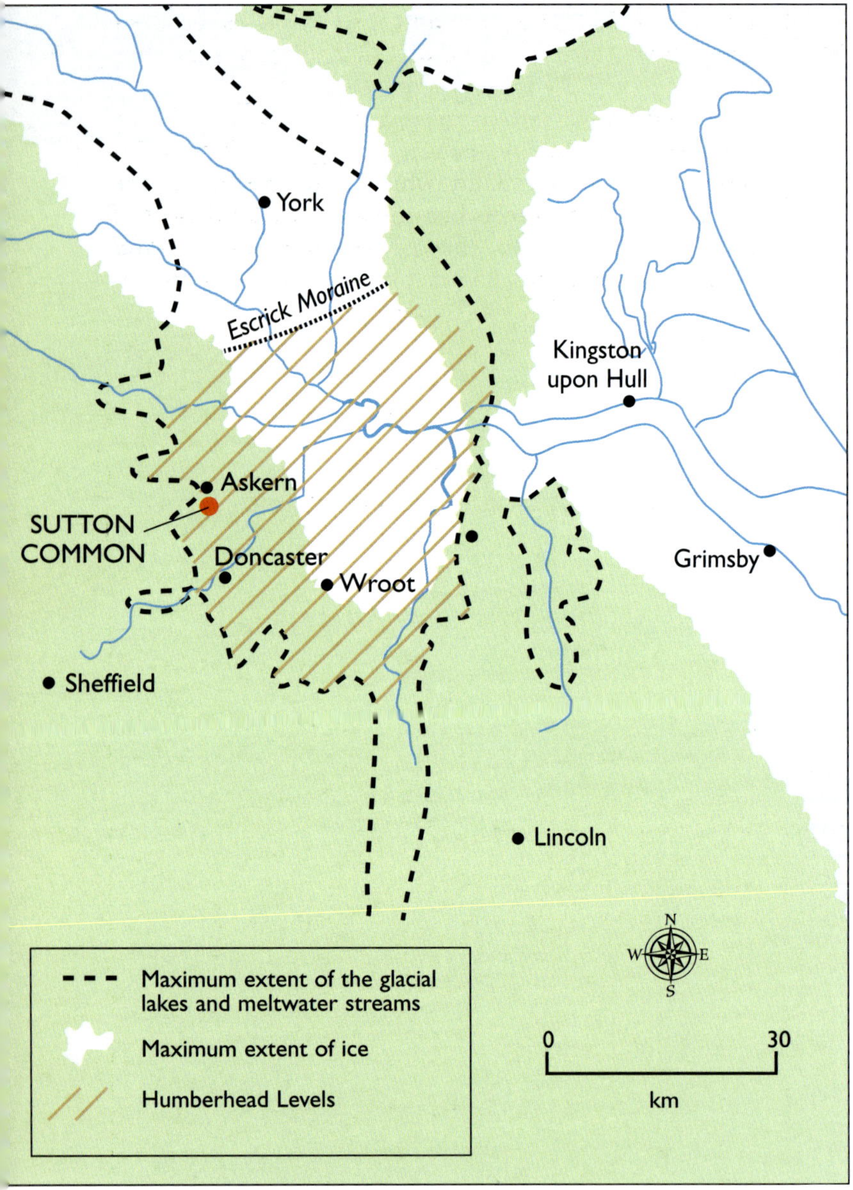
York
Escrick Moraine
Kingston
upon Hull
Askern
SUTTON
COMMON
Doncaster
Wroot
Grimsby
Sheffield
Lincoln
N
W
E
S
Maximum extent of the glacial
lakes and meltwater streams
Maximum extent of ice
Humberhead Levels
0
30
km

Lake Humber lay at the head of the ice front as it retreated.

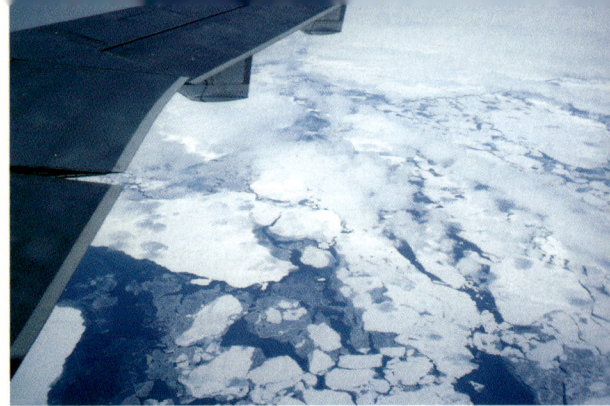

Ice floes over a lake on the edge of the polar ice sheet, today.

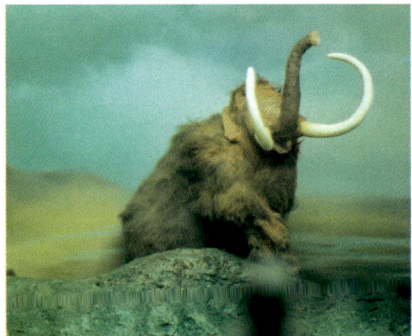

With the retreat of the ice from c.13,000 years ago large mammals such as the mammoth became extinct in Britain.

DONCASTER
MUSEUM
AND ART
GALLERY

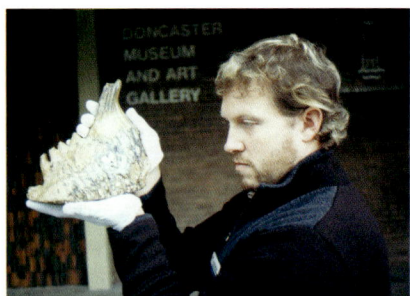

Peter Robinson of Doncaster Museum with a mammoth's tooth.

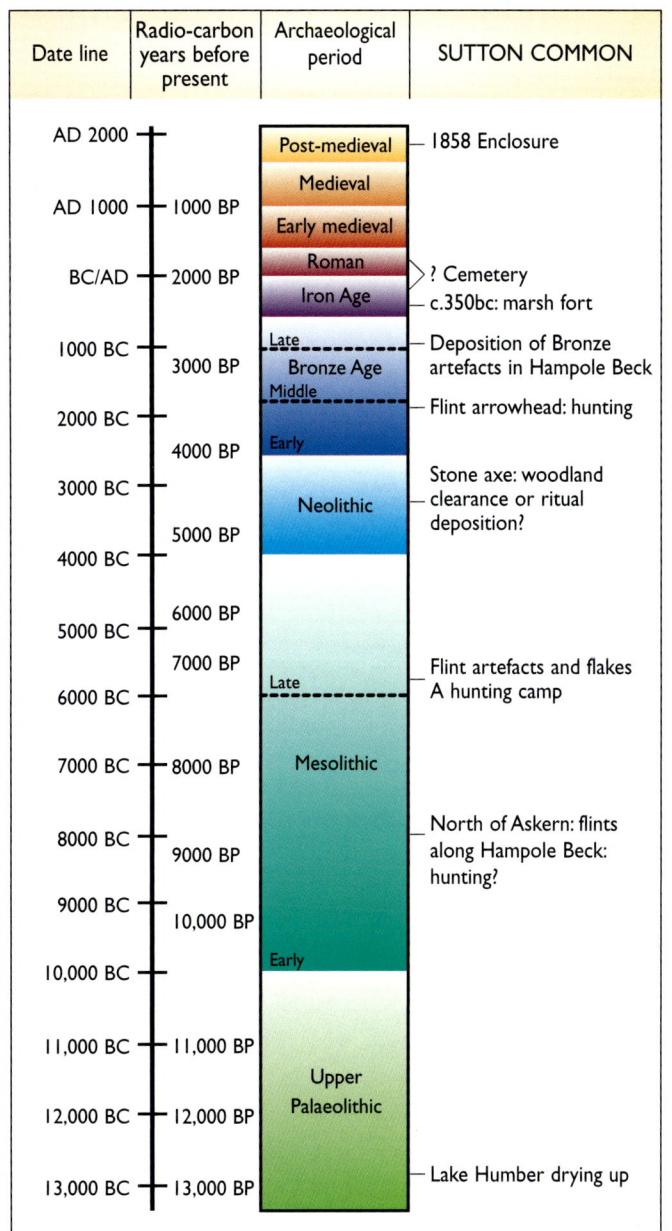

Date line	Radio-carbon years before present	Archaeological period	SUTTON COMMON
AD 2000		Post-medieval	1858 Enclosure
AD 1000	1000 BP	Medieval	
		Early medieval	
BC/AD	2000 BP	Roman	? Cemetery
		Iron Age	c.350bc: marsh fort
1000 BC	3000 BP	Late Bronze Age	Deposition of Bronze artefacts in Hampole Beck
2000 BC	4000 BP	Middle	Flint arrowhead: hunting
3000 BC	5000 BP	Early Neolithic	Stone axe: woodland clearance or ritual deposition?
4000 BC			
5000 BC	6000 BP		
6000 BC	7000 BP	Late	Flint artefacts and flakes A hunting camp
7000 BC	8000 BP	Mesolithic	
8000 BC	9000 BP		North of Askern: flints along Hampole Beck: hunting?
9000 BC	10,000 BP		
10,000 BC		Early	
11,000 BC	11,000 BP		
12,000 BC	12,000 BP	Upper Palaeolithic	
13,000 BC	13,000 BP		Lake Humber drying up

our area – the Went, Don and Aire – established their early drainage patterns across the emergent plain.

As the effects of the ice sheets lessened and the climate warmed up, the vegetation changed dramatically. The barren frozen land which had existed in the shadow of the ice sheets became a tundra landscape of mosses and low scrub – like present day Siberia – and then open grassland, roamed by large animals such as mammoth, reindeer and giant Irish deer, along with predators such as wolf, arctic fox and bear. As the warming continued, the larger herd animals were replaced by elk, red and roe deer and wild ox (aurochs). Then, from around 10,200 years ago, the grassland vegetation gave way to woodland as trees – which had been forced to migrate southwards into Europe to avoid the cold – began to re-colonise the land.

During this period, the area of the English Channel and the North Sea up to the Dogger Bank would have been a large area of dry land, connecting Britain to the continent. This was due to the fact that much of the earth's water was locked up in the great ice sheets covering North America and Europe, with the result that sea levels were up to 20 metres lower at the end of the last glacial period than they are today. Subsequently, as the ice sheets melted, the rising waters covered the North Sea plain, and around 6000BC (8000 years ago), Britain was finally separated from the continent. Sea levels eventually reached the equivalent of today's by about 1000 BC, approximately 3000 years ago.

Throughout this time, from the Mesolithic (Middle Stone Age) period, through to the Iron Age when the marshland fort on Sutton Common was constructed, human activity helped to shape the landscape. From the small-scale clearing and burning of reeds by

Mesolithic hunter-gatherers, to the larger-scale forest clearances and farming activities of the later Bronze Age and Iron Age settlers, humans have consistently adapted the natural environment to suit their needs.

And – crucially for us – these people left traces of their activities, not only in the form of settlements, burial sites and stray artefacts, but in the impact they had on their environment. The story of the changing landscape, and of human activity in it, is revealed through palaeo-environmental research – the study of past environments. A key part of this research is the study of plant remains, and especially pollen, recovered from buried waterlogged deposits such as the peats and organic-rich muds which fill the old river channels of our region.

Due to the exceptional preservation afforded by waterlogged deposits, Sutton Common and other wetland sites in our region are especially valuable resources for understanding past landscape developments and climate change, because of the palaeo-environmental evidence they contain.

WATERLOGGING

Waterlogging is the saturation of soil with water so that the groundwater table rises close to the surface. Water saturation fills all air spaces in the soil and this results in an absence of oxygen in the soil (also known as anaerobic conditions). This absence of oxygen inhibits the 'normal' biological and chemical processes which are responsible for the decay of dead organic matter, and thus waterlogging can lead to the long-term preservation of organic archaeological remains, such as the timbers from Sutton Common.

The following account draws on the latest research in this field to trace the changes that have taken place here since the end of the last Ice Age.

THE MESOLITHIC PERIOD (C.8,000 - 4000BC)

Evidence from sites elsewhere in Yorkshire suggests that during the earlier part of the post-glacial period (about 10,200-9000 years ago), as the climate improved, downy birch trees expanded rapidly into the region. The old channels of rivers such as the Went begin to fill with sediments, and the deposits of plant material recovered from these rivers and streams indicate that grasses, sedges, birch, willow, hazel and pine progressively colonised the landscape.

An ancient channel of the Hampole Beck (known as a 'palaeo-channel') which runs between the sandhills used for the Iron Age enclosures at Sutton Common formed a tributary of the River Went in this period. It is particularly clear from the air, and can be recognised on the ground from the peaty soil and lusher plant growth. Recent investigations have shown that it began to become infilled in the late-glacial period or soon after, at around 11,000 years ago.

At this time, the first tree or shrub species to colonise the landscape around Sutton Common were birch and willow, with fen communities of sedges and grasses occupying the wet areas around the channel. Pollen analysis of the palaeo-channel sediments suggests the presence of open birch woodland and grassland on the drier soils away from the channel. As we move further into the Mesolithic period, around 10,000-9500 years ago, hazel and pine start colonising the birch woodlands.

Research on other sites in the Humberhead Levels and the Vale of Pickering north east of York shows that,

Oaks colonised the drier ground.

As we might expect, the changes in the vegetation at the end of the last Ice Age were accompanied by changes in the types of animals that were available to the hunters. Instead of the large herd animals of the grasslands, like reindeer and giant Irish deer, some of which became extinct in the new warmer climates, smaller species more suited to survival in wooded environments became more abundant.

Red and roe deer, aurochs (an extinct wild ox), wild pig, elk, wolves and beaver are typical species found in the newly-developing deciduous forests of this period. To what extent these particular species were hunted by Mesolithic people here is hard to say, as finds of animal bone are rare on sites of this period in our region, and evidence for dwellings is rarer still.

One of the main difficulties that we have in recovering evidence for these earlier human groups is the masking of the earlier land surfaces – and the archaeological sites on it – by overlying deposits of later sediments. In particular, in the Humberhead Levels to the south of the rivers Aire and Ouse, the development of extensive peatlands from the Bronze Age onwards covers archaeological sites of earlier date. The more recent deliberate flooding from the rivers Trent and Ouse in the eighteenth and nineteenth centuries to create rich and fertile 'warplands' has had a similar affect, burying the medieval and earlier land surfaces beneath layers of silt.

Archaeological evidence is therefore most visible where the older land surface breaks through the overlying sediments, such as on the sandhills at Sutton Common. These areas, on the edge of the paleao-channel of the Hampole Beck to the north-west of the Iron Age enclosures, have produced the earliest evidence of human activity here, dating from about 6,000-8,000 years ago, during the Mesolithic or

along with the trees, there were herbaceous plants such as dock, plantains, thrift or mugwort, parsley and dropwort or meadowsweet. Then, between 9500 and 6300 years ago, as the climate continued to warm, mixed deciduous woodlands spread across the landscape, with trees such as elm and oak in evidence. Within the local region, pine is prevalent on the sand and gravel terraces adjacent to the river floodplains, and willow in the Trent floodplain.

PEATLANDS

Peat is what is left from plants which have died in waterlogged conditions. The absence of oxygen in such an environment leads to the partial decay and partial survival of roots, stems and leaves. Through the accumulation of layer on layer of peat, peatlands are formed, which are often known as mires. There are a number of different types of mires, such as blanket mires and the raised mires of Thorne and Hatfield Moors. Both of these receive only rainwater, and are therefore poor in nutrients. Sphagnum mosses which thrive in such conditions are the dominant species.

Middle Stone Age. The material, all of worked flint, includes an arrowhead, small blades, and four scrapers. There are also a number of flint 'cores' and flakes – evidence that the flint was worked here, that is, it was carefully struck and chipped into artefacts.

Despite the problems of interpreting such partial evidence – when parts of the site still lie buried beneath later sediments – the finds suggest that Mesolithic hunter-gatherers were using these low sandhills on the Common for seasonal camps, though whether they visited this spot just occasionally or returned here regularly over a long period – maybe several centuries – is impossible to say without closer investigation into the buried deposits.

Other Mesolithic finds have been made further north along the old course of the Hampole Beck and alongside the River Went at Moorends. This fits the pattern seen elsewhere in the region, where Mesolithic and later prehistoric flints indicating hunter-gatherer activity have been found alongside rivers. Sites similar to the one on Sutton Common have been found on the floodplains of the rivers Derwent, Torne, Idle, Aire and Trent.

The population of this corner of north-west Europe (Britain then still being part of the continental land-mass) would have been only a few hundred at any one time, living by hunting, fishing and gathering wild plants for food and materials. The communities in our region were able to exploit an extremely rich and increasingly diverse landscape, ranging from upland hills to lowland marsh, with plentiful rivers, streams and freshwater lakes. Sites elsewhere in Britain and northern Europe have yielded evidence for fishing, and hunting deer, elk, wild ox and pig, and of the use of a wide range of plants, including hazel nuts, water-chestnuts, goosefoot, sorrel, water lily, raspberry, apple, meadowsweet and acorns. However, in reality between 200 and 400 species of edible plants were potentially available for use by Mesolithic peoples.

Perhaps the hardest thing for us to do, given the limited range of plant and animal species we now use, is to realise just how rich the environment was between 10,000 and 6000 years ago. We are all too often influenced by images of hunters and gatherers in modern, marginal and impoverished situations, which do not really provide us with an accurate picture of the prehistoric past.

Indeed, given the richness of the environment in the Mesolithic period, it is perhaps surprising that, around 6000 years ago, prehistoric people began to change their exploitation strategies towards the use of domesticated animals and plants. This change is taken by archaeologists to mark the start of the Neolithic, or New Stone Age, period in Britain.

THE NEOLITHIC PERIOD (4000 – 2200BC)
AND BRONZE AGE (2200 – 700BC)

The Neolithic period (about 6000-4200 years ago) began with the arrival of the first farmers from the continent, bringing with them the first domesticated sheep, pigs, goats and cattle, and cultivated plants, including cereal crops. Using tools of stone, wood, antler and bone, the Neolithic communities created clearings for small farmsteads and built substantial ceremonial monuments in the landscape.

Evidence for Neolithic activity varies throughout the region. There is no suggestion that agriculture was taken up wholesale or that permanent settlements were established. It is clear that the rate of adoption of domesticated animals and crops varied both here and across the country as a whole. What evidence there is suggests that when the farmers had depleted the soil, they moved on to create new settlements. Alongside the development of agriculture, wild foods and other materials continued to be exploited. In this region, for instance, rivers continued to act as foci for hunting and gathering, fishing and fowling well into the later Neolithic and Bronze Age. Some communities may have continued living a largely hunter-gatherer way of life well into this later period.

While evidence for permanent settlement here is lacking, there is no lack of evidence for the permanent monuments which Neolithic people built. Most notable are the large ceremonial and funerary structures, like the henges and communal burial tombs that can still be seen in the Peak District and Yorkshire Wolds. They are also known from the nearby limestone ridge, where a long barrow burial mound known as King Hengist Long Rein still stands near Sprotborough, but most such sites in this rich farmland area have been ploughed level and survive now only as buried features.

These Neolithic monuments, made of stone, earth and timber, represent massive commitments of communal effort and resources, and were often created and used over many generations. They are especially significant for their emphasis on community, both in their construction and their collective use – for instance in the burial of many individuals together, often with their remains mixed together.

In the lowland areas such earthwork sites are rare, but we know from the finds of stone axes and flint blades that Neolithic people were active in the Humberhead Levels. The finds suggest that, as in the Mesolithic period, activity was concentrated on the rivers and riverside areas. At Sutton Common, the sandhills and site of the later fort alongside the former Hampole Beck have produced a number of Neolithic flint blades, and nearby is the findspot of the fine Neolithic flint axe, mentioned in the Introduction. Such axes of flint and other stone were made in large numbers and traded widely across Neolithic Britain. They were certainly capable of felling trees, and would have made formidable weapons, but in many cases the lack of wear on the axes suggests they also served as ceremonial objects and possibly as trading 'currency'.

The finds from the Common do not indicate settlement here, and it seems likely that the Neolithic peoples'

A Neolithic flint axe-head.

Darker green and brown patches in the vegetation and soil trace the braided course of the prehistoric channel (palaeo-channel) of the Hampole Beck.

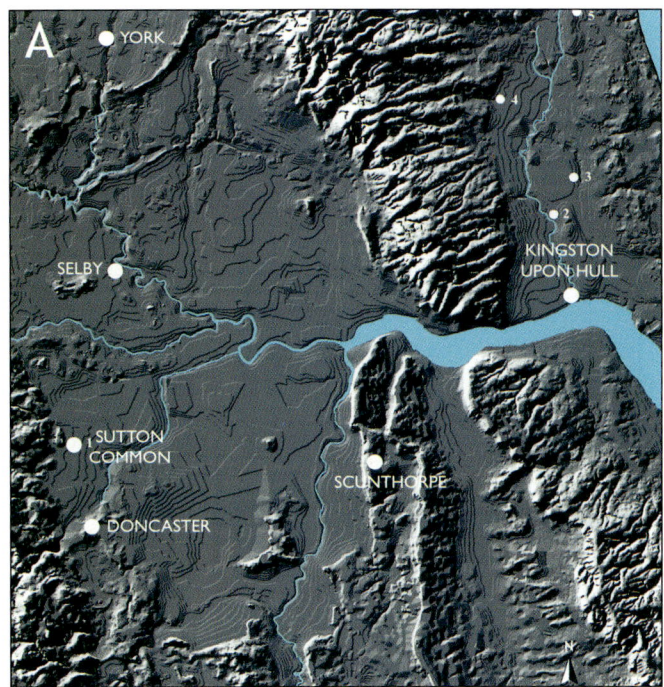

The Humberhead Levels today, lie in the area covered by the lake which formed as the ice melted and retreated after the last Ice Age and shows clearly on this digital elevation map of the area between Scunthorpe, Doncaster and just south of York.

Bronze Age flint arrowhead from the slopes of the large enclosure.

farmsteads and tombs were on higher ground to the west, and that they used this lower, wetter area for its natural resources – for hunting and gathering wild plants and as grazing land for their animals.

The transition to the Bronze Age, like the earlier transition to the Neolithic, was a gradual one. The agricultural landscape continued to expand in the earlier Bronze Age. Pastoralism was important, but wheat, barley and other crops were also cultivated. There now appears to be a shift in emphasis away from the community (as seen in the Neolithic) towards an emphasis on the individual, especially seen in burials, with bodies often now placed under separate round barrow mounds, sometimes grouped in cemeteries which may have acted as markers for territorial grazing rights. Towards the later Bronze

Age, settlements become more permanent, and changing traditions in metalworking, burial and pottery suggests that communities were placing new importance on the region and the household group.

The palaeo-environmental evidence charts the changes in the landscape during the later prehistoric period. Perhaps the most important elements of the Neolithic and Bronze Age landscape of the Humberhead Levels are the raised moors of Thorne and Hatfield, two of the largest surviving areas of lowland raised mire peatland in England. Peat mires such as these are especially significant to our understanding of the historic environment because of their potential to preserve waterlogged archaeological and environmental remains. The present moors represent only a fraction of the former extent of the peatlands.

Thorne and Hatfield Moors are remnants of the raised mires which covered once large parts of the lowlying areas of the Humberhead levels.

Common, investigations of the waterlogged infill of the Hampole Beck palaeo-channel and of the adjacent organic layers around the two Iron Age enclosures provide a picture of the vegetation. The pollen evidence indicates an open landscape dominated by grasslands and sedges, with some suggestion of alder carr vegetation around the site.

Perhaps the most important find is the presence of agricultural 'indicators' from plants such as ribwort plantain, found with cereal pollen of the oat/wheat group, and of rye and the plants from which it came. These discoveries support the idea that agricultural landscapes with cultivated 'fields' occur close to the Common in the later part of the Bronze Age or Iron Age periods, at a time when we know the people of the region were constructing the enclosures at Sutton Common.

Not only have large areas been dug for peat or colonised for farming, but the northern, western and eastern margins of the former moors are now buried beneath the relatively recent river sediments, known locally as warp deposits.

As we move forward in time to the period when the Iron Age enclosures at Sutton Common would have been in use, the evidence is that the clearance of woodlands continued. Areas of meadow and pasture are present, but similarities to the earlier Bronze Age landscapes are suggested by the continued presence of mixed fen woodland, grassland and reedswamp in the Vale of York to the north.

At this time in the Humberhead Levels, lime trees become less prominent in woodlands, and the moors of Thorne and Hatfield develop raised mire vegetation, dominated by sedges and heather. At Sutton

MALCOLM LILLIE

Malcolm is a lecturer in archaeology at the University of Hull, and was director of the Wetland Archaeology and Environments Research Centre for three years between 2000-2003. After working in the commercial side of field archaeology Malcolm obtained his first degree in archaeology from the University of Nottingham in 1991, and obtained an MSc and PhD from the University of Sheffield during postgraduate studies between 1991-8. He is currently course director for the BSc geography and archaeology programme at Hull, with an MSc in landscape archaeology scheduled to commence in 2004.

CHAPTER TWO

FROM FIRST FARMERS TO FLAGSHIP

The 2,500-year history of Sutton Common since the Iron Age presents a snapshot of the history of the whole of lowland Britain, as **KEITH MILLER** of English Heritage explains in this whistle-stop tour.

Now for a rapid journey through time, from the Iron Age enclosures, through medieval meadows, to the present-day pastures in the shadow of the former mining village of Askern. Fasten your safety belts, because this is about 200 years a page.

THE LATE BRONZE AND IRON AGES (1000BC-AD50)

The Sutton Common marsh-fort fitted into a wider pattern of late prehistoric land use. It lay on the margin of the limestone ridge running north through Askern, with its fertile, well-drained soils, and the neighbouring lowlands of the Humberhead Levels, with their heavier soils and denser natural vegetation. The limestone slopes, easy to clear and cultivate, became increasingly settled by farming communities, as did the drier areas in the Levels, ideally suited for pastoral farming and exploitation of the rich wetlands.

Long before the Romans arrived, there was already a well-developed pattern of farming settlements linked by roads and rivers.

Until the early Iron Age, the Sutton Common area was probably only used for seasonal camps and herdsmen's shelters rather than permanent settlement. The land here would have provided good hunting and fishing, and grazing for sheep and cattle in the drier months, and the marshes and wet woodland 'carrs' would have been an important source of raw materials such as willows, rushes and reeds.

Then, around 380-340BC, in the mid Iron Age, the fort was built. Representing a considerable investment of time and effort, it would have been an important focal point for the community. It was probably intended to serve a combination of functions – defensive, ceremonial, religious, social and economic. These various aspects are shown, for instance, by the evidence for ritual activity there, the fact that the ramparts are partly defensive and partly for show, and the use of the site for a cemetery after the fort itself had fallen out of use. Whether it was the presence of the earthworks, or something else about the place, the site was clearly still regarded as special.

The nearby wetlands, with its pools of dark peaty water and lush marshland vegetation, its low mists and eerie, flickering will o' the wisp lights (caused by natural methane marsh-gas), may well have had religious significance. Ritual offerings of Bronze and Iron Age weapons have been found in wetlands, and although nothing quite like this has been found at Sutton Common, some of the discoveries here, like the alignments of timber posts running out from the large enclosure towards Shirley Pool, and the skull burial at the entrance facing the marsh, hint at the possibility of ritual activity linked to the wetland. There is, too, the intriguing record from the early 1900s of a 'wooden shield' found in a brickyard claypit not far away.

Part of a broken Roman bangle found on Sutton Common.

THE ROMAN PERIOD
(AD43 – AROUND AD425)

The Roman army landed in southern England in AD43, and *Britannia* was soon established as a province of the Roman Empire. For many years the Roman frontier ran just to the south of our region, but a rebellion by the local Brigantes tribe prompted the Romans to push northwards. By about AD70 the army had reached Doncaster, where they established a series of military forts along the main road to York, later to become the Great North Road, and still visible in its early form as the Roman Ridge at Adwick-le-Street (named after the Roman 'street'). One of the campaign forts was nearby at Burghwallis,

while Doncaster (the Roman *Danum*) housed a permanent garrison.

Military conquest was soon followed by civilian settlement and the development of a 'Romanised' landscape of market towns and farms ranging from large villas to small 'native' farmsteads, and industrial sites like the potteries at Rossington and Cantley, which at one time supplied much of northern Britain.

The few Roman finds from around Sutton Common suggests that the area was outside the main area of activity which, as in earlier periods, was focused on the drier land to the west. It no doubt continued to be used for seasonal grazing and hunting. We can picture our site at that time, with the old walled ramparts and great timber structures of the fort gradually falling into decay, and the series of low burial mounds merging into the marshland vegetation.

THE MEDIEVAL PERIOD
(FIFTH TO FIFTEENTH CENTURIES)

The end of the Roman occupation – indeed of the Empire itself – came in the fifth century, under the impact of population movements sweeping across Asia and Europe. These brought people from the continent to settle in the British Isles: first the Anglo-Saxons and other tribes from the Low Countries, then the Scandinavians – especially the Danes – initially as Viking raiders and then as traders, farmers and settlers.

The new settlers had a major effect on commerce and development – seen most dramatically in the flourishing of Viking York and centres like the early riverside borough at Doncaster, with their trading links reaching far across Europe. Language and culture was strongly influenced too, and many settlements were either newly established or changed their name at this time.

The landscape was of course already mostly occupied, and some of the villages retained their earlier Anglo-Saxon names – like Sutton, Norton and Owston (the south, north and west *tons* or settlements, in relation to the main villages of Campsall and Burghwallis); Askern ('the house or corner where ash trees grew'); Moss ('the moss or marsh'), and Shirley ('bright glade or clearing'). But the many later Scandinavian place-names clearly indicate a major phase of new settlement and reorganisation of the farming landscape here between the ninth and eleventh centuries.

A look at the map reveals the Scandinavian impact in our area – in place names such as *ings* ('meadow'), *toft* ('building plot'), *carr* ('marsh') and *holme* ('water meadow' or 'raised ground in a marsh'), and village names like Carcroft ('farm in the carrs'), Adwick ('Adda's *wick* or farm') and Thorpe ('village').

Fifteenth century local landowner Robert de Haitfield and his wife, Aida, are remembered on a brass memorial in Owston parish church.

During this Anglo-Scandinavian period the earlier pattern of scattered farmsteads gave way to a landscape of villages and hamlets, each with their own field system. It was probably at this time that local communities organised the use of the marshlands here as village 'commons'.

With their conquest of England in 1066, the Normans took over a prosperous and well-organised country. Their Domesday Survey, undertaken in 1086, shows that the main villages in our area were Owston, Campsall, Burghwallis and Adwick. All still have Norman fabric in their churches, no doubt funded by the new Norman lords, whose nearby manor houses would have served as administrative centres for their estates.

Sutton (*Sutone*), which is listed in Domesday along with a lost settlement called Newhouse (*Newose*), was a small place with its own field system and a flour mill, all held by the Norman lord Ilbert de Lacy.

Domesday also gives us a glimpse of the farming landscape that was to last for the next eight hundred years. As in much of England, it was based on the 'townfield' system, in which each village or 'township' had its share of resources – arable land, meadows, common pastures, woodland and marsh, and sometimes fisheries in rivers and lakes.

In our area, the township territories were arranged so that each had a share of different types of land: the drier limestone slopes for arable fields around the villages, the lower land for meadows, and rough pasture and woodland 'commons' on the lowest, wettest moorlands in the east. Arable cultivation was in two or three large 'open' fields divided into numerous long narrow strips, each farmer's holding consisting of

several strips distributed around the fields. Farming was undertaken 'in common', that is communally, to ensure that planting, harvesting and grazing in the 'common fields and pastures' was done in an organised way.

Our site formed part of the extensive commons belonging to Sutton township, most of which lay in Campsall parish, with a small portion in Burghwallis. Around it were commons belonging to Owston, Askern, Campsall, Burghwallis and Haywood. Villagers' rights to the use of the commons were linked to the size of their property holdings. Top of the pecking order were the barons and lords of the manor with their own large holdings, then the peasant farmers and cottagers, each with several strips of land in the arable fields and meadows, and rights to share the use of the commons.

As in earlier times, the commons provided households with seasonal grazing land for cattle and sheep, and a

The age of grand designed landscapes. Illustrations by Humphrey Repton from his 'Red Book' for the nearby Owston Hall estate, show the landscape before (left) and as proposed (right). The lake in the centre was never created.

source of wood, willow osiers, rushes, and peat for use as fuel and a cheap building material. Shirley Pool may have been formed partly through early peat digging.

The use and upkeep of farmlands, commons, field boundaries and roads was controlled through local community by-laws or 'customs', and infringements were punished by fines levied in the manor courts. Grazing too many sheep or cattle on the common, or letting them stray into gardens or growing crops in the arable fields, meant a summons to court and payment of a fine to have the animals released from the village pound or pinfold.

Sutton Common was used in this way for hundreds of years, until its enclosure in 1858 – arguably the most dramatic and far-reaching change ever to have taken place here.

ENCLOSURE

In just a few decades, the regions's rural life and landscape were utterly transformed by enclosure (see box). Altogether, several thousand acres in the Askern area were swept up in Georgian Parliamentary Enclosures: at Owston, Adwick, Bentley and Thorpe in Balne in the 1760s; at Moss and Fenwick in 1779-83; and at Burghwallis, Campsall, Norton and Askern in 1813-18.

Sutton, however, was left out of these schemes. Whether this was due to issues of land ownership or economics, is not clear, but this small township of 730 acres and about 120 inhabitants remained unenclosed until 1858. In fact it was the last sizeable enclosure in the entire Humberhead Levels. Long after neighbouring areas had been drained and enclosed, Sutton's ancient arable fields were still being farmed in narrow strips, and its Common – with the earthworks of the marsh fort still clearly visible – was still being grazed according to community by-laws, a lone survivor of ancient unimproved lowland common land.

This was good for its archaeology, and it would also have served as a wildlife refuge, aiding the survival of rare species around Shirley Pool described by Tim Kohler in Chapter 8.

The original Sutton Enclosure document, now in Doncaster Archives, shows that most of the township was owned by local gentry, and describes how Sutton Common was carved up into new fields, given new drains and an access road, and allotted to the same leading landowners, who between them held most of the rights to the Common. Thus Philip Bryan Cooke of nearby Owston Hall, '…in respect of Ten Common Rights linked to Ten Village Messuages' (dwellings entitled to common rights), took the largest area of Sutton Common containing the prehistoric fort, listed simply as 'land parcel no.44, on the Far Common…' Frederick Bacon Frank and George Anne of Burghwallis Hall, lord of the manor of Sutton, took the adjoining areas, including Rushy Moor.

So, by 1858, Sutton Common and the surrounding area had been parcelled up and enclosed into a series of straight-sided fields flanking Shirley Wood, which was too low-lying to be drained for farmland. The new enclosure pattern survives especially well in the regular sequence of fields along Rockley Lane, just south of the Iron Age site.

Despite enclosure, most of this former common land was still too wet for arable and it remained as pasture and hay meadow, much as it had been in previous centuries. But it was not long before the new regime made an impact.

ENCLOSURE

The Enclosure Movement began in England in the late Middle Ages when village farmland was taken over by the larger landowners and converted to more profitable sheep pasture. It reached a peak between 1750 and 1850, when large parts of the country were enclosed by private agreement or Acts of Parliament, again usually on the initiative of leading landowners keen to consolidate their estates and take up more productive farming methods.

Through enclosure, the ancient communal townfield system of common fields and pastures was reorganised by land surveyors into a 'drawing-board' landscape of individual self-contained farms, with a regular layout of new fields enclosed by hedges and ditches. Common rights were privatised and converted into landholdings or cash payments and the land was redistributed. Scattered land holdings were amalgamated, and commons and moors regarded as 'waste' were 'improved' by being fenced and drained for more intensive agriculture. Along with the old field systems, many ancient tracks were abolished, and new roads and farmsteads appeared in what was previously open countryside, together with quarries, mines and other new industries. The resulting improvements in productivity had a lasting cost, both environmentally and socially. Following enclosure, most smallholders and cottagers gave up their holdings and worked on the larger farms or migrated to the towns, providing labour for the Industrial Revolution.

The pattern of enclosed fields still shows clearly to the left of Sutton village in the top right of this aerial photograph.

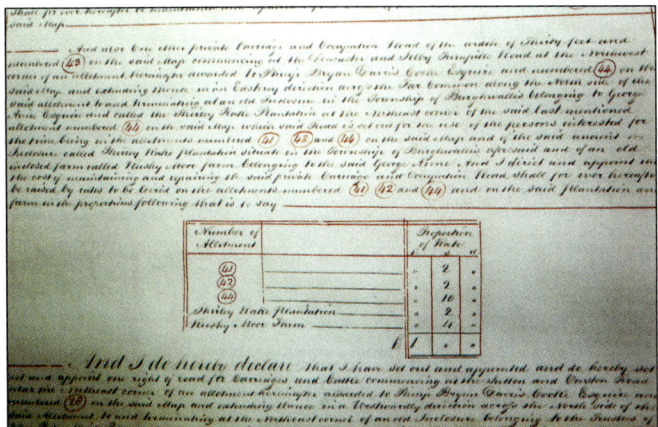

A section of the Sutton Enclosure award 1858 describes parcels of land at Sutton

The Enclosure Plan for Sutton Common shows a new track-way crossing east-west.

HISTORY DRAINING AWAY

Major drainage schemes had been undertaken in the Humberhead Levels in the seventeenth and eighteenth centuries, involving manipulating the rivers Don, Idle and Torne and cutting new waterways, like the Dutch River to Goole. These had a profound affect on the lowlands around Thorne and Isle of Axholme, transforming tens of thousands of acres of moors and commons to farmland, much to the annoyance of local people whose livelihood and economy were completely changed against their wishes. Though these schemes had little direct impact on the Askern area, they paved the way for local enclosure and drainage projects, and for subsequent agricultural and industrial development here.

The first signs that drainage was affecting Sutton Common came in the mid-nineteenth century. The first Ordnance Survey map of the area, published 1854, clearly depicts the two fort enclosures and labels them 'Crook Hills', presumably a local name referring to the irregular 'crooked' earthworks. Around this time, the Rev Scott Surtees made the first detailed record of the site. He saw timber stumps in the ground – long-buried Iron Age timbers that were becoming visible as the drainage of the neighbouring Commons began to take effect, drying out and shrinking the peat that had covered the archaeological remains.

Surtees reckoned the earthworks to be a Roman military camp. Others suggested it was a prehistoric site or a refuge for fugitives. Piece-meal excavations in the early 1900s, unfortunately poorly recorded, found a cobbled pathway, arrowheads, bones, timbers and thatch – the organic materials having been preserved in the waterlogged ground.

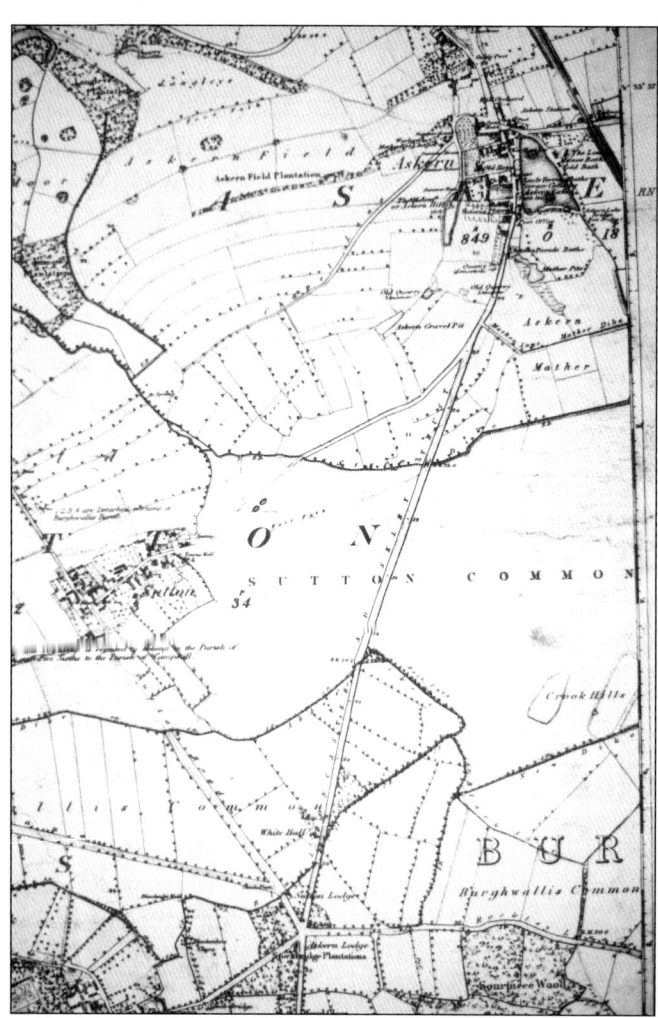

The first edition Ordnance Survey map of 1854 records the names of the enclosures as Crook Hills.

A wooden disk uncovered in the 1930s excavation and once thought to be a wheel, may well have been a vermin guard from the top of a granary support post.

The limestone western ramparts of the large enclosure, exposed during the 1930s excavation, were bulldozed flat in 1981.

More systematic excavations in the 1930s by Professor Whiting revealed further timber posts, walled ramparts, flint tools and wooden artefacts including a possible dug-out canoe and something thought to have been a wheel (see chapter 4). These rich archaeological discoveries led to the site being designated as a Scheduled Ancient Monument, to give it some degree of protection. All was well while the land was under seasonally-wet pasture, but from the 1960s onwards there was mounting pressure on farmers to expand arable production, and attention turned to the 'unimproved' areas of Sutton Common.

The protection of archaeological sites was then still in its infancy, and the limitations of the system were shown in 1980 when the large enclosure was bulldozed flat to convert the land to arable cultivation. Fortunately the work was spotted by one of the staff of Doncaster Museum on their way to work, and stopped in time to save most of the smaller enclosure. Ironically, this was just at the time when new legislation was being introduced to improve the protection of Ancient Monuments.

Then in 1982 the site received a second blow. The land drainage was intensified, partly in response to mining subsidence and partly again because of pressure for increased agricultural productivity. But this came with a high environmental cost: the waterlogged archaeological site and the Shirley Pool wetlands were now both seriously drying out.

Growing concerns about the situation led English Heritage to commission a series of archaeological assessments of the site in the 1980s and early 1990s by Sheffield University, the South Yorkshire Archaeological Service and Doncaster Museum. The most dramatic find from the Sheffield University programme of work was a wooden ladder from the

SCHEDULED MONUMENTS

Archaeological sites are often very vulnerable to accidental or deliberate damage, and need careful management if we are to pass them on to future generations. 'Scheduling' is the shorthand term for the legal system used by the government to protect and conserve nationally important sites in the UK. They are not necessarily very old, nor are they always visible above ground. They cover a wide range, from prehistoric cave dwellings, stone circles and burial mounds, to Roman forts, medieval castles and monasteries, early industrial structures and twentieth century military defences. Most scheduled monuments are privately owned, and English Heritage provides advice and grant aid to help with their conservation, management and interpretation.

The Sutton Common ladder – a notched pole – is on display in Doncaster Museum.

Sutton Common enclosures in 1976 before ploughing.

Sutton Common enclosures, in 1981 after the large enclosure had been bulldozed and ploughed and a corner of the small enclosure similarly damaged.

ditch of the small enclosure – the earliest-known example of a ladder in Britain, now in Doncaster Museum. According to one wit, we expected to find nearby the remains of the earliest-known window cleaner!

The investigations showed that, despite the bulldozing, the site still had enormous archaeological potential. But they also showed that the well-preserved waterlogged remains were deteriorating through 'desiccation' or drying out.

This work came at a time when there was growing recognition of the importance of wetland sites for preserving archaeological and environmental evidence which could not be found on dryland sites. To discover more about this valuable resource, English Heritage embarked on a series of major archaeological surveys of England's wetlands (see box). The last – and largest – of these surveys was the Humber Wetlands Project, based at Hull University in 1992-2001. Its coverage of the Humberhead Levels in 1995-6 included further assessment at Sutton Common, and paved the way for the current English Heritage-funded project being carried out by the same archaeologists, now at Exeter and Hull Universities, whose work is described in Chapters 3, 4 and 6.

The assessments confirmed that Sutton Common was continuing to dry out and deteriorate. If this continued, most of the rich organic deposits – the preserved wood and the plant material – would soon vanish. Massive timbers that had survived two thousand years were rapidly dwindling away, and would be gone within a generation.

There was no apparent way to remedy the problem. The large enclosure in particular was suffering – in

Robert Van de Noort explains to Bruce Keith of English Nature how wood that has survived for more than two thousand years has dried out and is now rapidly disappearing.

WETLAND ARCHAEOLOGY

The four national wetlands surveys conducted by English Heritage – in the Fens, the Somerset Levels, the North-West, and the Humber basin – have highlighted the incredible range and richness of wetland archaeology. And its vulnerability. Sutton Common is not alone – wetlands throughout the country are under serious threat from drainage and water abstraction, loss of pasture, peat extraction and building development. Over 10,000 wetland archaeological sites – about three-quarters of the known total – have been damaged or destroyed in the last 50 years. The work at Sutton Common has a vital role in helping to save what remains. The archaeological project here – the largest and most comprehensive programme of its kind – is leading the way in the study and conservation of wetland sites, and plays a key part in English Heritage's work in developing a national strategy for conserving and managing wetland archaeology.

future years there would still be an archaeological site, but it would be a dry husk, marooned in intensive farmland. Like a big ship ploughing ahead regardless, there seemed little chance of turning this situation around until it was too late, and the damage was done.

But, as this book describes, through close teamwork and generous partnership funding, not only has the ship been turned around, Sutton Common has itself become a flagship for archaeological and environmental conservation and community partnership.

In the process, the project that began with a single archaeological monument has now spread to encompass other sites, wildlife and the wider historic landscape. Rightly so, since conservation has to be totally integrated, and these are not separate things but aspects of a single multi-faceted environment. Adjoining Sutton Common, for instance, is Shirley Pool, with wetlands, woodland and peat deposits containing evidence of earlier landscapes. Alongside are archaeological sites – the sandhills with their early prehistoric finds, the Iron Age marsh-fort with its later cemetery, all set within former medieval Commons overlaid with a nineteenth-century Parliamentary Enclosure field pattern. Together this makes up a living landscape with a history stretching back thousands of years, and with traces of different historic periods still visible today.

And as well as linking through the local community and the wider scientific world, the work at Sutton Common has, in a very real and practical way, connected with other less obvious communities in this multi-layered landscape – the myriad species of flora and fauna in the local habitats, and the many generations of people who have used this place in the past. They too have now been given a voice.

Visitors explore the excavations.

KEITH MILLER

Keith Miller BA (Hons), Inspector of Ancient Monuments for English Heritage's Yorkshire Region, has spent nearly thirty years in the heritage profession in the Lincolnshire-Yorkshire area, working variously as a Sites and Monuments Record Officer for the Humberside Archaeology Unit, Listed Buildings Investigator for English Heritage, a heritage consultant, and an adult education and university lecturer in archaeology, landscape and architectural history. Keith advises on the management of several hundred historic monuments, providing advice on developments affecting them, and on grant-aided conservation and research programmes for the region's archaeology and the wider historic landscape.

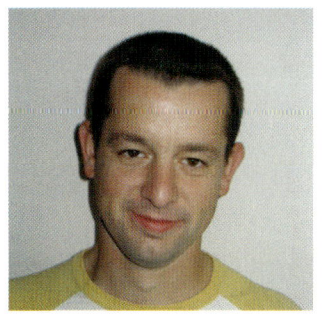

CHAPTER THREE

THROUGH TIME AND SPACE

Dog walkers on Sutton Common got used to the odd sight of **HENRY CHAPMAN** laden with his strange equipment. But *Time Team's* Henry, who reckoned he walked 22 miles and stood still for eight hours, obtained some fascinating and innovative results on the unseen landscapes of the common

When I was asked to undertake a survey of Sutton Common in 1997, it was a place I already knew well. Having worked in the region for a couple of years on the Humber Wetlands Project, I was well aware it was an important Iron Age site and I understood its archaeological significance as a rare wet-preserved landscape, with evidence of surviving timbers and other material. Hence, I was extremely happy to hear that it had been bought in order to save it. Finally, I thought, this important place might stand a chance.

The aim of the survey was simple, but its results, and the implications of those results, could not have been predicted. The intentions at that stage, in the autumn of 1997, were to generate a point-in-time assessment of the resource.

In other words, we were after a snap-shot of what was there on the surface which would enable two things to be addressed in the future. Firstly, it would be a record of the earthworks and landscape setting of the site as it was in 1997. Secondly, it would provide a starting point for all further investigations above and below ground.

Wetlands are more complicated than most types of archaeological site, both in terms of interpreting and managing them. The high water table restricts oxygen within the burial environment, meaning that the influences of the factors that destroy organic archaeology – fungi and bacteria – are limited or stopped. The importance of Sutton Common lay in the preserved organic archaeology; the wood and the peat that had been kept from harm for perhaps two and a half thousand years through a high water table.

A three-dimensional model of the surface archaeology would act as the bench mark against which fluctua-

WHAT IS GPS?

Global Positioning System is a US satellite-based technology for calculating location, currently used for a range of activities from firing missiles to in-car navigation. The technology uses a number of satellites which orbit around the planet sending radio frequency signals which can be received by GPS equipment. The information which is broadcast from the satellites records time delays, from which it is possible to calculate distance from the satellite to the receiver – using the known wave length and the time difference between broadcast and receipt. By receiving signals from at least four satellites , it is possible to triangulate the position of the receiver, in a similar way to triangulation on a map, but in three dimensions.

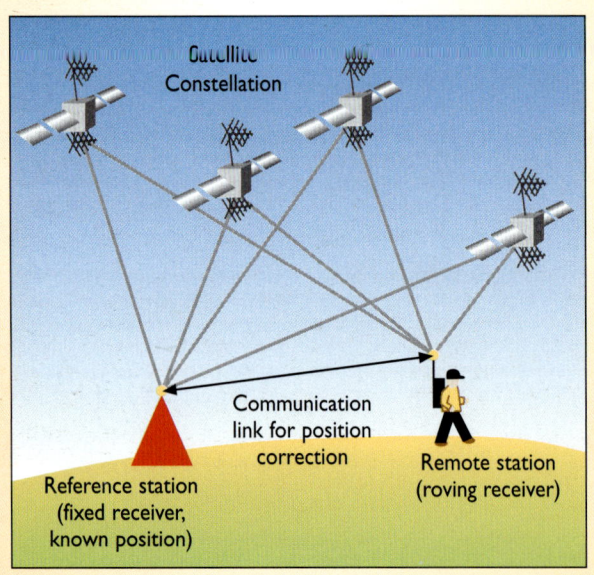

Satellite Constellation

Communication link for position correction

Reference station (fixed receiver, known position)

Remote station (roving receiver)

tions in the water table, and the three-dimensional positions of organic archaeological remains, could be measured. Only with this information would it be possible to manage the archaeological resource effectively. But this type of work was very new and ambitious, and we'd have to create the techniques and agenda as we went along.

At the time of surveying, computer modelling of archaeological sites in three dimensions was a very new thing. Contour maps had been made previously showing the heights of different parts of a site, but such an approach is very static and does not lend itself to comparison with other layers of data from other analyses.

We knew from the outset that a wetland site like this would require a more sophisticated approach. The potential of computers to generate 3D maps of parts of the landscape had been demonstrated by others, but was used very rarely, especially in relation to an area of this size. Normally much larger areas were studied in a much lower resolution based on commercially avail able data. For Sutton Common, we'd have to collect our own data, as it didn't exist in any other form.

However in 1997, the capability of surveying equipment was also subject to something of a revolution. The development of satellite-based high-accuracy surveying was beginning to take off – namely using GPS (Global Positioning System) equipment – the same technology which is now found in many cars and within hand-held navigation devices. We were in a position of using new surveying technology and new computer modelling technology together – a Brave New World for archaeology!

So 1997 forms something of a bench mark in the union between new approaches to computer mapping, new approaches to surveying to get data to put into the

Close-up of the GPS tripod-mounted base-station and roving hand-held staff.

Assembling the Global Positioning System (GPS) equipment.

computer, and the needs of a very special and significant wetland archaeological project – it just hadn't been done before. This meant that, not only was this survey aimed at quantifying the physical resource and levels of the site itself, but it also became an experiment in the applications of a new method within archaeological research. Good for the archaeology of Sutton Common, and equally beneficial for the progress of archaeological science.

We wanted to create a 3D computer model of the site, but to do this, a number of steps needed to be taken. Firstly, raw data appropriate for our purposes had to be obtained. At Sutton Common, this consisted of numerous three-dimensional positions recorded across the site, giving a position in space and a height above sea level for each location. Secondly, the resulting list of coordinates had to be loaded into the computer and processed to create a continuous virtual surface.

Essentially, it is like bending a sheet of rubber so that it passes through each of the surveyed coordinates, making educated guesses to calculate the likely pattern of the areas lying between the points. There are numerous ways of achieving this based on some quite weighty maths, and so some exploration needed to be undertaken. This resulting 'model' then forms the basis for a number of analyses, even before comparing it to other data sources.

So in the autumn of 1997, I set out from Hull University with some shiny new GPS surveying equipment, with the capability of measuring positions across the fields to a three-dimensional accuracy of within a centimetre. It was a strange time of year, with the evenings drawing in, and the eerie mist which gradually appeared within the old in-filled river channel. The common was quite a lonely place, with only the occasional dog-walker to chat to – or rather be quizzed by – about the strange staff and backpack which I was carrying around the field.

The equipment consisted of two parts, quite different in appearance but similar in function. A tripod was set up in the field with a large plastic dome on the top which collected signals from specialised satellites orbiting the Earth, unscrambling the data and transmitting it via radio to the second part of the equipment. This consisted of a metal staff with another plastic dome, also collecting signals from the satellites. This was attached to a backpack holding kit to unscramble these signals. The information from both parts of the equipment was processed in a small computer attached to the staff, calculating its position.

The survey consisted for the most part of taking position readings with the staff every five to ten metres across the common. The equipment I was using required the surveyor to hold the pole absolutely still for about five seconds in each position before moving on. You can probably imagine how this must have looked – walking perhaps eight paces, then stopping for five seconds to take a reading, and then walking another eight paces, and so on. And then, once I'd finished a strip, I had to walk back to record another line, or transect, parallel to the first, but five metres to one side. In some areas, such as the smaller of the two enclosures where the earthwork remains of the prehistoric enclosures were still obvious, the process became much more intense.

In order to collect enough data to create a representative computer model of these features I needed to record positions at a much higher resolution, sometimes at every metre, or less. Looking back over the data now, I have worked out that I walked well in

The Sutton Common Group gathered around the GPS equipment in the middle of the palaeo-channel in the early days – note the rushes growing in the wetter ground.

excess of 35 km (about 22 miles) up and down across the common just collecting positions.

For the whole site, I recorded nearly 6000 individual positions in this manner. This took most of five days of walking up and down, and stopping for five seconds to record each point. That works out at approximately 500 minutes (eight hours!) of just standing still, added to the time of walking. Things have become much quicker now, and I dread the thought of all that time that it took back then, although despite technological advances, the amount of walking remains the same. However, to put things into context, before this technology was available, it would have been unthinkable to perform such a survey. It is easy to forget how fortunate we were that the new techniques and equipment became available at the time.

After a week in the cold collecting data, the next step was to do something with the information I'd recorded. The processing of survey data is something that I always find exciting. You are never sure what will be churned out of the computer once your data is fed into it. It is easy to make too much of the anticipation, suffice to say that I was anxious about what the result might bring, and concerned that it would be useful. In the case of Sutton Common, the results were far more interesting than we could have imagined, providing much more than a snap-shot of the site against which to compare future data.

It is possible to display the three-dimensional computer models in a number of different ways. The most basic is perhaps a type of contour plot, with shades or colours graded to display changes in elevation. On the Sutton Common model it was immediately possible to understand the site in a way that really couldn't be appreciated on the ground.

MODELLING IN 3D

The technology of 'spatial information' is filtering through into a vast range of everyday experience for everyone, often without us realising it. Geographical Information Systems (GIS), the broader name for the discipline, has become fundamental to most areas of life, from calculating the best route in your car, to weather mapping and battlefield logistics. GIS relates to any kind of computer data basing that involves some spatial component, or location. This might be in two dimensions or three, depending on the requirements of the user.

Two 'islands' stood out above the lower wetland area – and these had been the focus of human activity over two and a half thousand years ago. Other smaller islands were visible that had been used over four thousand years ago, leaving the residue of tool-making activities. It was also possible to see the interaction of the old river channel running between these islands and the areas of archaeology. The falling land towards Shirley Pool was also obvious.

By applying analysis techniques to the computer model, even more remarkable information was gained. For example, a virtual light source can be applied to a 3D model which highlights subtle changes in the surface, a bit like the low sun in winter emphasising the contours of the land and features such as banks and ditches.

On the model of Sutton Common this technique showed many things. Firstly, the upstanding earthworks of the smaller enclosure were clearly visible – at

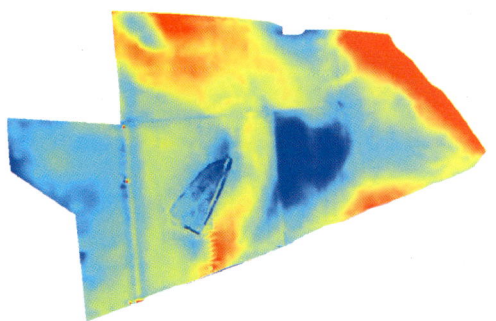

Colour shading by height.

Hill-shading to give 3-D effect.

Perspective comparisons.

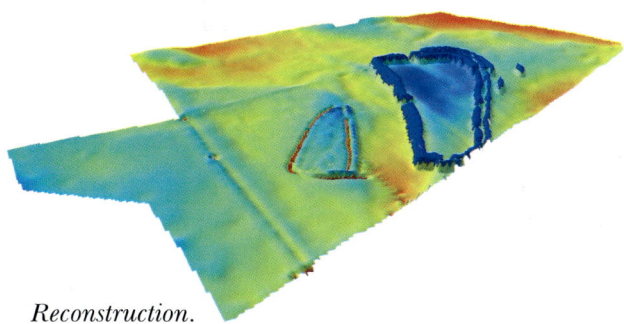

Reconstruction.

Assessing effects of raised water table.

The data recorded can reveal features invisible to the human eye and present them in many different ways.

the time of surveying, much of this area was covered by dense vegetation and so the earthworks couldn't be seen. Not only did this provide us with a picture of the archaeology, but also indicated the level of preservation of these features. Secondly, despite the bulldozing and ploughing of the larger enclosure, archaeological features could also still be seen. These were completely invisible on the ground. Particularly on its western edge, it was possible to identify the ancient ditch as a very slight depression running across the field.

What we were seeing on the model was scientifically very new. The ditch that was visible had been infilled with peaty soil which acts something like a sponge, expanding when saturated. Similarly, when peat is dried out, it shrinks. However, unlike a sponge, even if you get peat wet again, it will not re-expand – it has lost its structure. The depression on the model represented the shrinking of peat in the ditch below the surface, thereby causing the surface of the field overlying the ditch to drop very slightly.

In 1997, the common was covered in stubble, having been cropped for its last time. Ploughing will level off a field's surface, and the field had last been ploughed in the previous year. This meant that the peat shrinkage that was revealed by the ancient ditch had occurred within less than a year and thus had far-reaching implications.

Previous archaeologists had assumed that the archaeology of the larger enclosure was nearly dry, and hence organic remains such as wood would have been lost. The evidence from the model suggested the contrary. For the peat to still be shrinking suggested that there was still peat there to shrink, and thus potentially some organic archaeology. This also suggested that we'd just discovered a new method for finding archaeological sites within wetlands.

HENRY CHAPMAN

Dr Henry Chapman is the co-director of the archaeological research currently being undertaken on Sutton Common. He is based at the University of Hull, specialising in digital mapping and prehistoric archaeology, and is a regular specialist on the TV programme, *Time Team*. Henry is a graduate of the Universities of Exeter and Hull, and has previously worked for the Royal Commission on the Historical Monuments of England as a landscape investigator, and on wetland archaeology projects based in Hull.

CHAPTER FOUR

EXPLORING AN ENIGMA

When tales of 'Yorkshire's Ghost Village' hit the local Press, Sutton Common really started to get on the map. Here **ROBERT VAN de NOORT** of Exeter University, who led the two-year dig, explains how it probably wasn't really a village at all

Archaeological research on the Sutton Common enclosures goes back at least to the 1860s, when the Rev Scott Surtees mapped the site, interpreting the enclosures as the remains of a Roman military camp. Several other local enthusiasts visited and explored the area in the late nineteenth and early twentieth centuries, but not until Prof Whiting's excavations in the 1930s was it realised that the enclosures were probably of prehistoric date. It took nearly another 50 years, and only after the monument had been badly damaged by bulldozing, before new research was undertaken here.

Small-scale excavations carried out by the now defunct South Yorkshire Archaeology Unit, including Sheffield University and Doncaster Museum, in the 1980s and 90s retrieved some tantalising finds – including the earliest known ladder in Britain. They also highlighted the deteriorating condition of the site following drainage. However, in 1997, following the publication of a paper summarising all previous research, it was concluded that the function and nature of the Sutton Common earthworks was still unclear. The use of the term 'enclosure' didn't enlighten anyone, as archaeologists have many different meanings for that term. Suggestions that the place had been a fort, a settlement, a religious monument or a cattle range had all been considered and rejected. In short, Sutton Common was still an enigma.

Following the transfer of the ownership of Sutton Common to the Carstairs Countryside Trust in that same year, various plans were hatched aimed at resolving this enigma. After all, it was impossible to decide on the future management of the site and the Common if we didn't know what we were trying to preserve. Further research was required, and this included Henry Chapman's GPS survey of the land (explained in the preceding chapter), and small-scale excavations in 1998.

Up on the cherry picker.

The excavations seen from the cherry picker.

The defining moment came in 1999. In that year we had excavated the western gateway and a set of ten trenches over the larger enclosure. The results were spectacular, proving beyond any doubt that much of the Iron Age remains were still there, despite the bull-dozing in 1980. A Baldrick-style cunning plan was quickly devised.

We would invite English Heritage Chief Archaeologist David Miles to Sutton Common for a visit. We were going to hire a hydraulic platform, known as a 'cherry picker', which would give a bird's eye view of the excavations. This couldn't fail to impress even the most experienced archaeologist, and further support from English Heritage would, we hoped, be forthcoming.

On the morning of the visit, the cherry picker was positioned to provide the best possible view, overlooking the gateway. Fortunately, I decided to do a test run, only to get stuck halfway up with the cherry picker out of order. We tried everything to get it going again, but to no avail. My only way to get back on the ground was to jump onto the roof of our Landrover, so that I didn't have to shout down to the Chief Archaeologist.

Despite all this, David Miles was truly impressed, and even without a bird's eye view, he agreed to support our proposal for a large-scale excavation. When he and Keith Miller, the regional Inspector of Ancient Monuments, took the proposal to the English Heritage committee of Britain's leading archaeologists, they wholeheartedly backed the scheme and agreed to fund the excavations which took place in 2002 and 2003.

So it happened that English Heritage kindly provided the money to explore this enigma and to rescue vital archaeological evidence before it dried out and

Left: *An aerial photograph of the 2003 excavations, seen from the east. Note the minibus – the white dot – between the middle trenches.*

Below: *The 2002 trenches. Shirley Wood is in the foreground, Askern in the distance.*

The first stage – removing the ploughsoil.

Cleaning the surface of the trenches after the topsoil has been removed.

disappeared. That support provided us with the opportunity to follow one of my old professor's mantras: 'Don't excavate to answer any questions quickly, but excavate to leave no questions unanswered'.

Over two seasons, we excavated eight large trenches, together about the size of three football pitches. The even-numbered trenches were excavated in 2002, and the odd-numbered trenches in 2003. Joined together, the excavations revealed nearly the whole interior of the larger enclosure, where we expected to find the answers to the enigma, and about a quarter of its defences. It had been decided to leave the smaller enclosure untouched. After all, in these parts it is a very rare example of an upstanding prehistoric earthwork.

Once the ploughsoil had been removed by machines, the trenches were cleaned by hand, and all archaeological features were recorded on plans. At the Common, most features stand out as dark patches against the natural light sands and silts. Where these dark patches are small, they indicated the location of posts and stakes; where these are bigger, they represent pits, wells and ditches.

Following the planning of all these features, a selection was excavated. Sometimes we found the pointed end of a stake, or the flat-bottomed base of a post belonging to a structure, but most frequently we only found the discoloured soil, all that was left of the wooden object which once stood there. In the ditches, we found animal bones and peat, which will help us in understanding the economy and vegetation of the Iron Age.

We still have a long way to go before we are ready to publish the report with all the final conclusions. Much work is needed on the analysis of the plans, the animal bones and the peats. But we have now sufficient evidence to make some informed decisions what Sutton Common was all about.

Essentially, we think that Sutton Common was an Iron Age fort. In the world of archaeology, the word 'fort' means man-made defences principally comprising banks and ditches which enclose a settlement or other important ground. In Britain there are over 3,300 prehistoric forts. Most occupy the tops of hills (and thus are named 'hillforts'), but others have been found on hill slopes, on scarps, or in lowland situations.

Several Iron Age forts are located within wetland landscapes, notably in the East Anglian Fenlands and the mires in western England. We think that Sutton Common was something similar. In other words it was a defensive site, but in the absence of a suitable hill, the wetlands of Shirley Pool and the Hampole Beck were utilised to create a defensive setting for the fort. The term 'marsh-fort' seems therefore appropriate.

The principal reason for calling the Sutton Common enclosures a 'fort' is that their defences resemble that from many hillforts, both in Yorkshire and further afield. In fact, it would not be surprising (but impossible to prove) if the designs for the ramparts and gateways had been copied from somewhere else. On the basis of analogies with hillforts in England, a mid-Iron Age date of, say, 350 BC could tentatively be assigned to the Sutton Common marsh-fort.

Cleaning the base of posts from a section of the box rampart.

The defences consisted of a so-called box rampart, encircling the larger enclosure, formed from two parallel rows of posts, 2.5m apart, with planks or roundwood timbers placed on the inside and filled with earth, creating a solid wall of 2m or more high. The box rampart was entirely uniform, and only interrupted for the eastern and western gate. Outside this box rampart was a ditch, and beyond this a low bank with a stockade through the centre, adding to the defensive character, especially if these stakes had been sharpened at their tops. A second ditch lay outside this bank.

The two gateways were most imposing, and we believe that they were designed as much to impress those who entered the site as to contribute to its fortification. In fact, some features of this design suggest that the military character of the site was not as important as its ceremonial function.

The smaller enclosure was essentially an elaborate entranceway, with people in the Iron Age approaching

Even a small section of a gateway post needs a JCB to lift it – how did its builders handle them when they were 4m long?

from the drier land in the direction of Owston. The smaller enclosure was linked to the larger one by a causeway across the wetlands of the Hampole Beck. This causeway would have been of crucial importance as a defence in times of war, but instead of building a narrow, easily-defendable causeway, this one was no less than 9m wide. Again, it seems that the site has been designed as much to impress as to function as a real 'fort'.

Inside the defences of the large enclosure, we found numerous posts and post holes, in addition to a single well and various pits. The overwhelming majority of posts and post holes turned out to be something we call 'four post structures' or 'granaries' (see box). We know now that some 150 of these structures stood in

the larger enclosure. But to everyone's surprise, we didn't find a single house.

So what was Sutton Common? We believe it was essentially a marsh-fort with ample storage facilities. It was built using the same architecture and presumably for the same reasons as many hillforts over much of Britain in the Iron Age, but rather than positioning the fort on top of a hill, the impenetrable marshes were used for best effect. Why people never lived here, or never lived here for any length of time, is something harder to fathom. But I can make some informed guesses here too.

Archaeologists have debated for some time the concept of 'cosmology', that is the ancient belief of

Describing and recording all of the archaeological features is vital and an exacting, time-consuming job.

FOUR-POSTERS

This photograph of a four-post structure was taken during a family holiday in Northern Spain. It is a granary and examples of these structures can be found at virtually every farm along Spain's north coast. This part of Spain is known as the Costa Verde, or green coast, because of the abundant rainfall. The granaries date back to the fifteenth century, but are still in use as food stores and new ones are frequently built.

The reasons for this are simple. The structure is designed to keep food dry, and avoid the problems of rising damp. Also, if accidental fires spread from the house or kitchen, they would not effect the vital food store. And thirdly, vermin is much less likely to come into the house if there is no food available. The stone 'disks' on the posts are there to prevent mice and rats from climbing into the granary. During the excavations at Sutton Common in the 1930s, archaeologists found what was thought to be a wooden 'wheel' in one of the ditches. This 'wheel' may well have been used in a similar way as the stone discs seen on the Spanish four-post structures.

A granary in northern Spain. Stone disks at the top of the legs stop vermin from climbing into the food store. Could the Sutton Common site have been filled with 150 of such structures?

THE SUTTON COMMON 'GHOST TOWN'

During the 2002 excavations, the national press was out in force to interview the excavators of Yorkshire's 'ghost village'. To be honest, we never suggested that Sutton Common was a ghost village. However, I did say to a journalist that digging Sutton Common felt just like digging a ghost town because we had found lots of structures but nothing, such as houses, that proved that people had ever lived here. Of course, the papers, radio and television thought it was a great story, and even friends in Holland heard the story of the Iron Age ghost village that was being excavated at Sutton Common.

The press take an interest.

systems or set ways in which certain things are understood to have to be done. In the Iron Age, this cosmology included the concept of living within enclosed, defendable settlements as an ideal, even though the actual threat of hostilities from neighbouring tribes may have been very small. Not only that, but the way in which this was to be achieved followed clear rules, understood by all involved.

First the defences had to be completed. Second the storage facilities were constructed and used. And third, houses would be built and people moved to live within the fort. However, in many instances the second or third phase was never completed, and the fort as an enclosed settlement remained only an ideal. This cosmology existed across Britain, and this explains why many other hillforts are effectively empty shells, devoid of any evidence for any habitation, while a few others have granaries but no houses within their defences.

We can think of several reasons why Sutton Common never turned into a proper settlement. It may have been the case that the site was simply meant to be a model or ideal, or was found to be too impractical by the farmers who worked their land on the limestone ridge to the west. The analysis of pollen from within the ditches and the old channel of the Hampole Beck suggest that after the defences had been constructed, the area became wetter, and this could have triggered the decline of the marsh-fort.

Alternatively, the granaries may not have functioned properly in the humid wetlands, and some evidence for this is forthcoming from the analysis of the burnt grain we found here. But whatever halted this development, we should not forget the enormous amounts of energy and material that was needed to construct the site.

A considerable time after the marsh-fort had been abandoned, probably towards the end of the Iron Age, people started to visit it again. This time it was not for any military reasons, but for the burial of cremated human remains which were placed within small areas enclosed by narrow ditches.

Evidence of a cemetery. The bases of small c.3m funerary enclosures.

MURDER ON THE COMMON?

The laws of England require archaeologists to inform the local coroner when they find human remains. Thus when we found a human skull in one of the ditch terminals near the easternmost gateway, I duly rang the Doncaster Coroner. He immediately sent a CID officer to investigate the case. When he found that the victim was at least 2000 years old, and the culprit beyond prosecution, he relaxed somewhat, but nevertheless wanted to know exactly what had happened here. I explained to him that human remains, especially skulls, were often used in the Iron Age to signify entrances. We don't know whether these were the heads of enemies or of their own ancestors, but it is clear that certain 'magical' properties were associated with them. The deposition of skulls and other objects in ditch terminals near entranceways is fairly common in Iron Age Britain, and conforms to their cosmology. A colleague visiting the site and having been told that we had found the previous week a human skull in one of the four ditch terminals near the eastern gateway, could pinpoint the exact location immediately. He explained that human skulls in ditch terminals in British hillforts are always found to the north of the entranceways. We can therefore assume that the symbolic meaning of placing skulls in ditch terminals was understood by all those who saw it.

This practice is not well known from Britain at all, and it took us a long time to realise what we were uncovering. Of great interest in this context is that the people who buried their dead at Sutton Common clearly recognised the by-now ancient marsh-fort as a place that connected them with their ancestors.

All in all, by rescuing the remains and resolving the Sutton Common enigma, and also discovering a very rare late Iron Age cemetery, we have fully justified English Heritage's support for the excavations. And what about cherry pickers? We never used another one. Instead, in 2002 and 2003 the Trust hired a helicopter for us to get a true bird's eye view of the excavation, and for some stunning aerial photography. With repeated circuits, everyone working on site had a memorable impression of their handiwork...and nobody got stuck.

An alternative to a cherry picker.

ROBERT VAN DE NOORT

Robert Van de Noort (BA, Drs, FSA) studied history at the University of Utrecht and archaeology at the University of Amsterdam. He worked at the British School at Rome and the Rotterdam Archaeological Unit before coming to England in 1992, where he became the Project Manager of the English Heritage-funded Humber Wetlands Project and Director of the Centre for Wetland Archaeology, based at the University of Hull. In 2000, he became Senior Lecturer in Archaeology at the University of Exeter, where he has directed several English Heritage projects into the future conservation management of England's wetlands. Robert's principle research interest is in the archaeology of wetlands.

CHAPTER FIVE

PRESERVING A PERCH

One of the most rewarding and fascinating aspects of the archaeology at Sutton Common was the involvement of local schoolchilden in a 'burying your lunch' project, conducted by English Heritage's **IAN PANTER**. He describes the unique experiment here.

It was with a certain degree of trepidation that a small team of us assembled at the Miners' Welfare, Askern, waiting for the first school group to arrive with their packed lunches. Mark Anthony-like, we were going to ask them not to eat their lunches, but to bury them, subject to scientific recording at Sutton Common.

This was September 2000, the start of the 'Rubbish and Archaeology' project, originally conceived by Robert Van de Noort of Exeter University and Mike Corfield, then Chief Scientist for English Heritage. I was the local man on the ground and took over the organisation of the project while Mike was safe in his office, 200 miles to the south.

What was the aim of Rubbish and Archaeology? To quote from our official project design:
> *... the aim of the project is to encourage the people of Askern, and particularly the young people, to become partners in the future care and management of Sutton Common. In order to achieve this we propose to develop programmes in experimental archaeology and undertake scientific research into the deterioration of organic and inorganic remains through an experimental burial project with archaeological researchers and local schoolchildren participating side-by-side".*

In other words we were going to carry out experimental archaeology and attempt to demonstrate to over 150 youngsters what archaeology is all about, especially how artefacts survive burial. We also hoped to raise awareness of a more topical concern, that of waste disposal – what happens to all the rubbish that we throw away today, and will any of it survive for future archaeologists to discover?

As with all successful operations, a great deal of planning was necessary and essential groundwork was required for the project to succeed. First of all we had to ensure that the three schools in the Askern catchment area (Askern Junior, Norton Junior and Campsmount) were prepared to release their students to us. We also had to ensure that the schoolchildren were aware of what we were trying to achieve and what we wanted them to do.

At this point I thought it wise to bring on board Julie Ward, Education Officer for English Heritage, who knew all about dealing with large numbers of schoolchildren. We took time to visit each school and discuss the project with the students and staff. Many of them were aware of the ongoing work at Sutton Common, and many of them had watched *Time Team* on TV, so knew a little about archaeology.

Together we hit upon the idea of producing 'lunch boxes', dividing each class into small groups. Each student was responsible for providing an item of food or a utensil that might be found in a lunch box. We were hoping for a wide range of materials (having dropped strong clues during our talks) and we were not disappointed.

The schoolchildren put a lot of thought into the project, and the items provided included both cooked and raw chicken drumsticks, meat pies, fruit, cakes, half-eaten sandwiches, full and empty packets of crisps and peanuts, half-eaten chocolate bars (I suspect that

The perch.

Mike Corfield, then Chief Scientist for English Heritage, demonstrates the use of the video microscope to record surface details prior to burial.

some of these were surreptitiously consumed during the walk from school to the Miners' Welfare), fruit juice cartons, the ubiquitous fizzy drink can, as well as packaging, cutlery and other types of containers. If we were to award a prize for the best item though then it would have to go to the lad who went out and caught a small perch. I didn't enquire too closely about where it came from.

At the same time as the students were collecting their lunch boxes, the team of archaeologists given the task of supervising the work (from Exeter University and English Heritage) were putting together an assortment of archaeological replicates that would be recorded and buried at the same time. These included replica Iron Age ceramic pots, rush baskets, copper buckles and coins, wheat grains, lamb joints and wooden stakes.

Each item was subjected to a battery of tests both prior to and after burial in order that any change in condition could be measured. The tests were designed to cover a broad spectrum of characteristics which might

SNACK ATTACK

The most often-heard response from children asked to bring in an item from a lunch box was: "But I have school dinners, sir."

be expected to change while the object was buried, and the children gained experience in using a range of scientific techniques and equipment. Simple descriptions of each item were entered into a notebook produced for the project. These were complimented by sketch drawings, dimensions and volume measurements (calculated by the water displacement method).

Finally, the children brought their items to the Miners' Welfare where we had established our 'laboratory' in the salubrious surroundings of the bingo hall. The original intention was to run the entire operation from a marquee set up on Sutton Common. For logistical reasons, the Miners' Welfare proved more successful.

Further measurements included digital photography, surface microscopy (using a video microscope which transmitted the enlarged surface image onto a TV monitor), moisture content (using a meter developed for the timber-drying industry) as well as scientific colour measurement, using a chromameter. This device operates by firing a xenon light at the surface of an object and recording how much light is reflected. I'm sure that never before had so many tests been performed on such a collection of items!

Once all tests were completed, the material was then ready for burial. Sutton Common is an excellent choice for projects of this nature as there are both waterlogged and dry soils at the same location. Waterlogged soils tend to favour the preservation of organic materials due to the lack of oxygen and reduced microbial activity. Fungi and bacteria are the principal agents of decay of organic matter, but most can't function at low oxygen and high water levels. We could anticipate a better degree of preservation for the foodstuffs buried in the waterlogged zone.

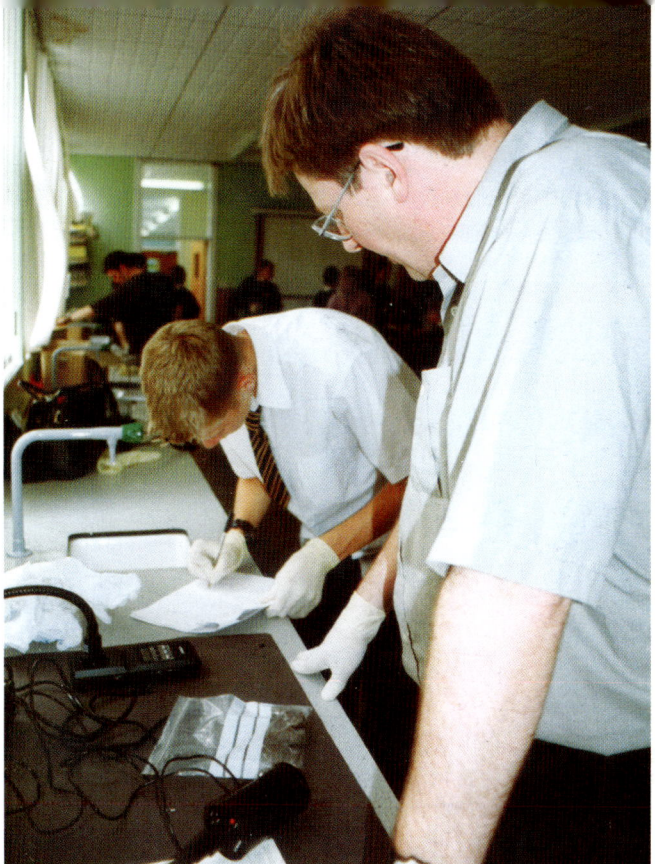

Changes to colour were scientifically measured before and after burial using a chromamater for comparison with students' own interpretations.

The students get ready to bury their lunches.

A grid in the base of the dry pit enabled the location of each item to be recorded before being covered over and left.

The wet pit.

However the reverse would be expected from the dry zone; as these soils are well aerated with high levels of microbial activity, the foodstuffs should decay very rapidly. Water and oxygen in combination create a very corrosive environment for metals, and again, comparisons between the two burial environments would be interesting. We also asked each student to hazard a guess as to what might happen to their item, and record their ideas in the notebooks.

Four pits were opened: two in the waterlogged peat deposits and two into the drier clay soils, and each pit was dug to a depth of about 0.5m, or just below the water table in the peaty areas. All the waste items were labeled and bagged in inert garden netting and placed into the pits. Each pit was gridded so that we could record the precise location for every item. One of our main worries that we would lose items didn't materialize, but it's better to be safe than sorry.

The original intention had been to dig up everything during the course of the following year, but unfortunately Foot and Mouth Disease intervened and all site work was halted. It was not until the following spring that we were able to gain access to the land and continue with the experiments. We thought this might prove to be a blessing as it meant that the material had been buried for almost two years as opposed to the original six months and would, hopefully have suffered more decay. Another concern of ours was that a six-month burial period would be too short for any effect to be observed in many of the items.

Another 'occurrence' proceeding burial also had an influence. The devastating floods of the winter of 2000 were also experienced at Sutton Common, with standing water over much of the common for approximately two weeks. Therefore our plan to investigate

Torrential rain caused a serious flood, seen here from the air, which complicated the experiment.

The flood from the ground.

the effects of two opposing burial environments was scuppered almost immediately.

Despite all these trials and tribulations though, it was with enormous relief that almost two years later we returned with a small group of schoolchildren from Campsmount School (by this time all 152 pupils had progressed on to secondary school at Campsmount) and re-opened the original pits. Not only were we able to successfully locate the pits, but also almost all the items were recovered.

For Health and Safety reasons, everything recovered was immediately sealed in a clear polythene bag, with the intention being to complete the post-burial recording with the material still in its bag. Through

the assistance of Paul Simmons, Head of Science at Campsmount School, we were able to commandeer one of the science labs, and then, over the course of one week, we completed the recording, using the same methods and techniques applied before burial.

So what did we discover about the durability of our materials?

Not surprisingly, the plastic-based items had undergone little or no change whatsoever (it has been suggested that some plastics in landfill sites may take over 450 years to breakdown – future generations of archaeologists will be better placed at understanding past cultures from the well-preserved material remains). Almost all items that were plastic coated (such as paper drink cartons) also survived intact, although usually crushed by the weight of the soil overburden, forcing the liquid out to drain away in the soil.

Metal cans fared much worse though, with all examples suffering severe corrosion, particularly along joints in the containers. There was no discernible difference between cans buried in the 'waterlogged' trench and those in the 'dry' trench, which indicates that both oxygen and water were available to provide the impetus for corrosion. However, the copper alloy buckles and 'coins' buried as archaeological replicates were not so heavily corroded, and most examples exhibited only a slight surface tarnish.

The presence of oxygen also accounts for the severity of decay seen with the majority of food materials, although preservation was marginally better in the waterlogged pits. Nothing organic was recovered from the dry pits, although the bone from a chicken drumstick survived. The structure of bone consists of a mineral component sheathing an organic compo-

A LASTING EFFECT

One popular brand of 'fruit juice' had remained inside its plasticized carton, and following filtering to remove sediment, proved still to be drinkable, although I personally cannot vouch for its taste and quality! I'm convinced though that this is testament to the power and strength of the preservatives applied to food and drink these days.

NB: No one has suffered from any strange disease as a result of taking part in the experiments.

nent, and it is probable that the organic element (collagen) had decayed, but the simple tests carried out by the schoolchildren weren't designed to detect such complex decay.

Of interest though was the nature of the decay of the foodstuffs buried in the waterlogged pit. While it was evident that the majority of the food items had been digested by microbial activity before low oxygen conditions (anoxia) had been established, elements of the food had survived. Once such example was an apple, where the fleshy inside and core had rotted away entirely, but the outer skin had remained. Clearly the outer skin was more decay resistant, but whether this is due to a more resistant structure or the presence of an applied preservative remains to be seen. Similar examples were seen with a cheese sandwich, where the white bread had rotted entirely but the cheese still survived, and according to one source, still had a 'cheesy' odour to it. It has been proposed that the survival of the cheese can be attributed to its high fat content.

And what about the perch? Besides the bones and part of the eye, (which caused much amusement back in the school labs) very little survived. Virtually all the fleshier parts had rotted away, although traces might have remained in the mixture of soil and peat around the bones. Along with the lamb joints, the perch now resides at Exeter University awaiting further detailed analysis.

Our simple experiments have demonstrated that the conditions necessary for preserving organic materials were not established in time to prevent the onset of decay of our perishable items. It is possible that these items were simply too vulnerable to survive, and that only in exceptional conditions will we ever find traces of meals eaten by our ancestors.

Preservation depends upon the creation of an anoxic burial environment, one where microbial activity is retarded or halted through the exclusion of oxygen. Decay never ceases entirely though, but anaerobic bacteria (bacteria that live in oxygen free environments) operate at a much reduced level than their aerobic counterparts. Therefore anaerobic decay is almost imperceptible and it's possible for perishable foodstuffs to survive. The discovery of a reputed Tudor banana skin from an excavation in London is testament to this. Maybe our pits weren't of sufficient depth and that oxygenated groundwater was constantly percolating through both the peat and clay soils.

If we were to undertake the experiments again, then burying at a greater depth would prove informative. The time factor will be important too, and running the experiments again, but this time keeping to a short six-month period would, I suspect, provide us with very useful data concerning initial decay processes. The longer than expected delay, brought about by Foot and Mouth, had more of an influence than we originally anticipated. Field experiments are always at risk from unexpected factors.

But the experiments have served their purpose. The local youngsters have become involved in the ongoing archaeological work at Sutton Common, and they have learnt much more about archaeology from their hands-on experiences. The project also gave them the opportunity to work outside the school environment and undertake tasks that they might never experience at school. And, dare I say it, it also allowed them to rub shoulders with the experts, and indeed *vice versa*, for the experts also learned by rubbing shoulders with the students.

Furthermore, the results will have brought home the realities of modern waste disposal, that plastics really do take an extraordinary length of time to disintegrate. While archaeologists of the future might have an easier job of interpreting the evidence, what sort of landscape are they going to be excavating? Mountains of plastic?

One final point – a project of this nature only succeeds through the good will and energy of everyone taking part. A big thank you must go to the teams from Exeter University and English Heritage, but most importantly to the pupils and staff from the three schools concerned. Everyone kept smiling throughout, even when the rains came down.

IAN PANTER

Ian graduated from the Institute of Archaeology, University of London, with a degree in archaeological conservation and material science. His previous jobs include the Mary Rose Trust, Portsmouth City Museums and the York Archaeological Trust. He is now employed as the archaeological science advisor for English Heritage (Yorkshire region) and has developed an interest in reburial and the *in situ* preservation of archaeology.

CHAPTER SIX

USING SCIENCE TO SAVE THE SITE

The life of a research archaeologist is not all roses, as **JAMES CHEETHAM** discovered. His ground-breaking work at Sutton Common not only decided the optimum conditions for the underground presevation of artefacts, it also imparted a healthy respect for thistles… and cows.

It is no overstatement to say that I have a deep fascination with and a very strong affinity for Sutton Common. Not only has it revealed many wonders to me academically since the late 1990s, but it has also affected me on a more personal and fundamental level as well.

For example, when you excavate a worked piece of wood and are able to touch the axe marks for the first time since they were created almost 2500 years ago, it gives you a direct connection to the person who actually made them, and you can't help wondering who they were and what their lives were like. In essence, you bring them alive and realise that they are the same as you in all aspects, except time.

I first experienced this on Sutton Common during the 1998 trial excavation undertaken by the University of Hull. Soon after I was offered the opportunity to continue my involvement through research aimed at

Uncovering a huge oak post in the edge of the causeway between the enclosures.

understanding the conditions within the burial environment of the archaeological materials still preserved there.

This involved extensive monitoring of the site through various means, including soil chemistry and measuring the activity of soil micro-organisms, as well as the research which focussed on monitoring the watertable.

Saturation is the single factor that dictates whether wooden and other organic materials, which hold such detailed information about the people who constructed the site, survive for the future or break down into nothing more than brown earth. When soil is in a waterlogged environment, the air is excluded. This means that all the micro-organisms that cause degradation are also inhibited. Having a saturated burial environment does not necessarily imply perfect preservation, but a lack of it definitely means the destruction of organic archaeological remains.

Monitoring of the water table was carried out using a regular network of fifty pieces of equipment called piezometers. The network covered both of the archaeological enclosures, the old river channel separating these, and extended towards Shirley Wood.

From September 1998, I started monitoring the piezometer grid regularly every two weeks. Although used to undertaking field work, up to this point I was something of a 'fair weather academic' and was not prepared for some of the conditions that I would be subjected to in my attempts to maintain activity through a regular monitoring period. In 1998 Sutton Common had not long been out of cultivation and the vegetation was in the process of recovery. At that time I experienced few problems finding each of the piezometers. However, the following spring brought drastic changes and I was rudely introduced to the prickly nature of the thistle during my regular 2.5 km/ 1½ mile walk through these plants, which often approached six feet in height.

The water table data obtained from the piezometer grid were used to create a virtual surface using Geographical Information System (GIS) software. We know where the piezometers are located within the grid, and the depth at which the water in them is, so it is possible to generate point data relating to the three-dimensional spatial location of the water table throughout the grid. The GIS takes this information and generates a surface which represents the location of the watertable.

Despite the problems with the rampant thistles, the gathering of data on the water table was proceeding well, and was already revealing some of the mysteries of the dynamics of the site that had not previously been observed either here or anywhere else.

For a start, it was becoming increasingly obvious that the water table was very strongly influenced by seasonal changes, as during the winter the water table was relatively high but in the summer this situation reversed, and the water level dropped significantly. Although this was to be expected on Sutton Common, at no time in the past had this process been quantified and observed at such a high resolution. Perhaps more importantly, the variation in the form of the water table across the monitored area had never been understood in such detail.

As the monitoring progressed, it became clear that the wetness of the site was influenced by the balance between the amount of rainfall received and the amount that removed from the ground by the surface vegetation. During the summer months when the

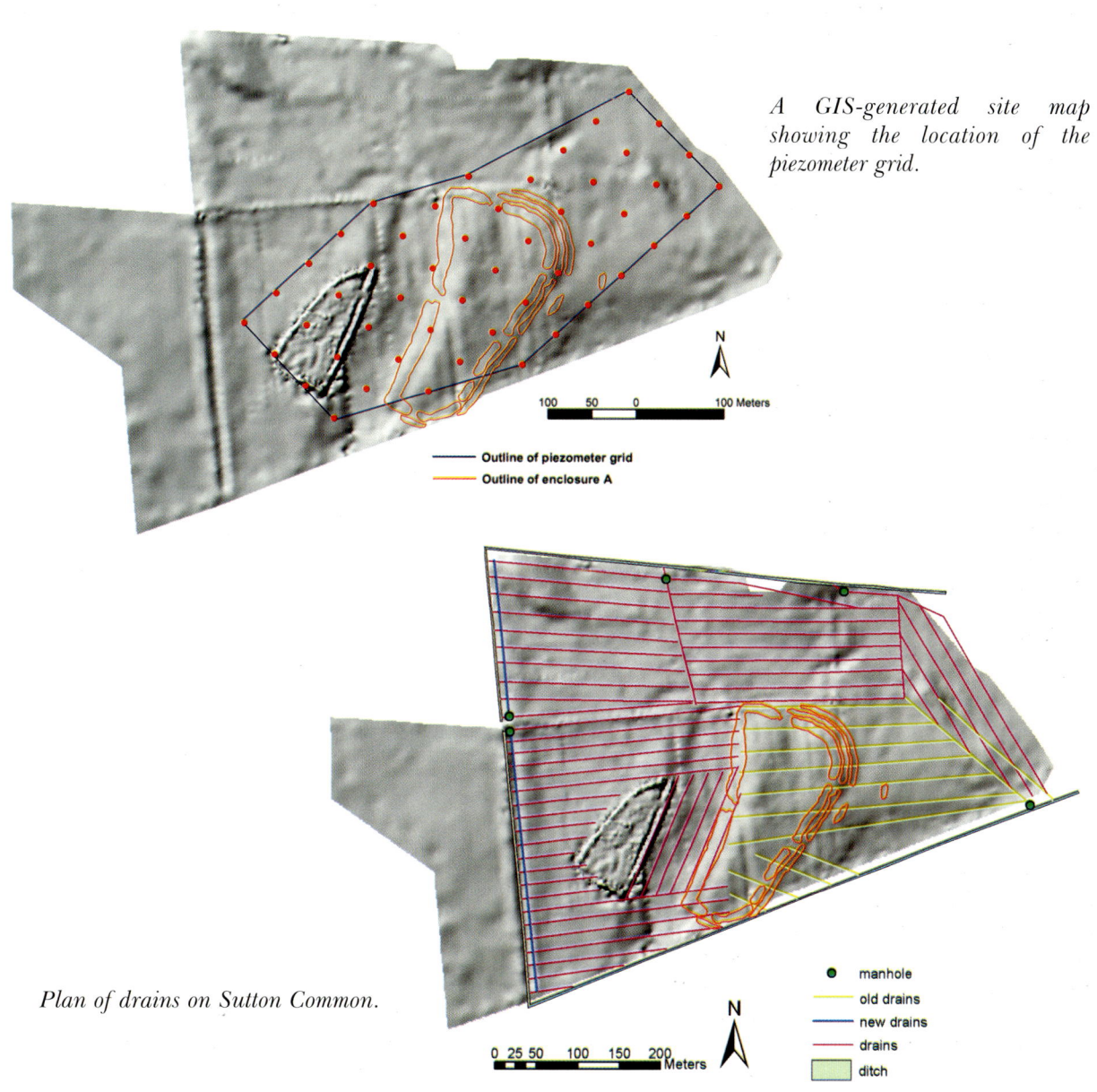

A GIS-generated site map showing the location of the piezometer grid.

Outline of piezometer grid
Outline of enclosure A

Plan of drains on Sutton Common.

manhole
old drains
new drains
drains
ditch

Demonstrating how to take a piezometer reading to Jan Knowlson, the then Chairman of CCT.

PRINCIPLES OF A PIEZOMETER

A piezometer is a plastic tube sealed along its entire length, with a perforated tip at the end to allow the free flow of water. The tip contains a screen to prevent the tube becoming blocked with soil over time. This is driven into the ground to the desired depth. Piezometers are designed to measure 'hydraulic head', this being the sum of two separate properties – the pressure head and elevation head. The point of measurement of a piezometer is at the buried, perforated end and water rises up the tube due to the water pressure within the ground. This is called the pressure head. The height at which the piezometer tip is above a known height is called the elevation head. In situations where there are no layers that are impermeable to the flow of water between the piezometer tip and the ground surface, piezometers measure the upper level of saturation, or in other words, the water table.

The tip of a piezometer.

weather is dry and vegetation growth is at its greatest, there is a lack of water in the ground, which is termed a Soil Moisture Deficit. During this time, water is progressively removed from deeper below ground and as a consequence the water table falls.

I experienced great changes in the seasons, with recorded temperature ranges of between -4 and +36 deg C. On one winter morning I was forced to abandon monitoring the piezometers, as every one that I came to had the cap pushed off by a column of ice.

Sutton Common had developed a habit of catching me out at the earliest opportunity. In October 1999, I decided to drive my vehicle out to the location where I was working, to save time transporting the necessary equipment. Everything was fine until I attempted to drive back, at which point the van promptly became stuck.

After four hours of trying every trick I knew from jacking the car to laying bucketfuls of gravel in front of the tyres, I had achieved nothing more than moving the vehicle a couple of feet in the wrong direction – and covering myself from head to foot in mud. I conceded defeat and phoned the university for help, which duly arrived an hour later in the form of the departmental Landrover. To this day I cannot fathom how I drove in, but got stuck while retracing my route out – it was almost as if I had fallen into a trap!

There were also times when Sutton Common was kind to me. During another visit to the site, I realised about half way through monitoring that the van keys were no longer in my pocket. After a quick and rather panicky phone call I confirmed my worst fears – that I had been in possession of the only keys in existence. Looking back across the acres of tall vegetation, I had visions of being stranded. However, after retracing

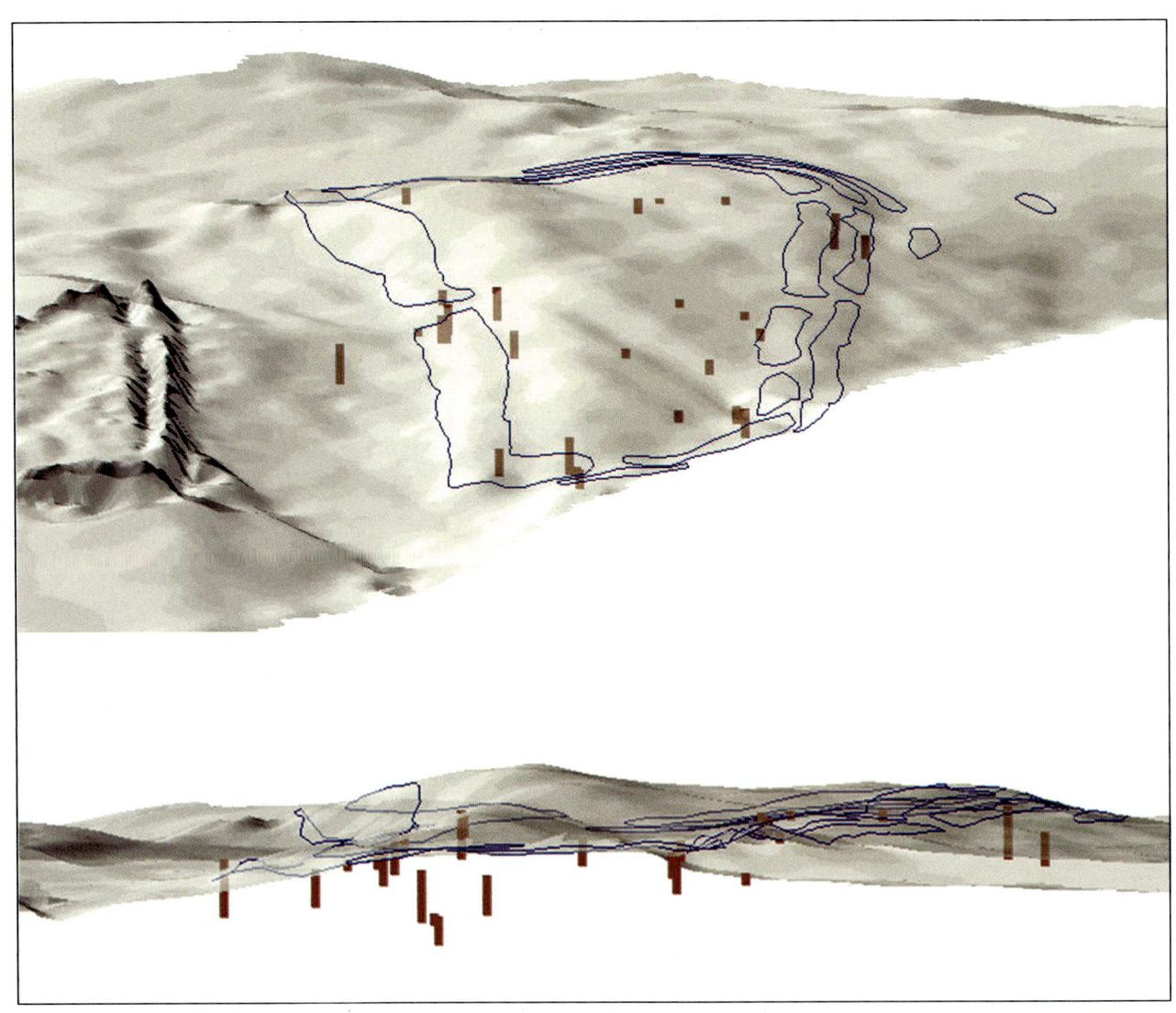

The locations of known archaeological wood and its depth within the common.

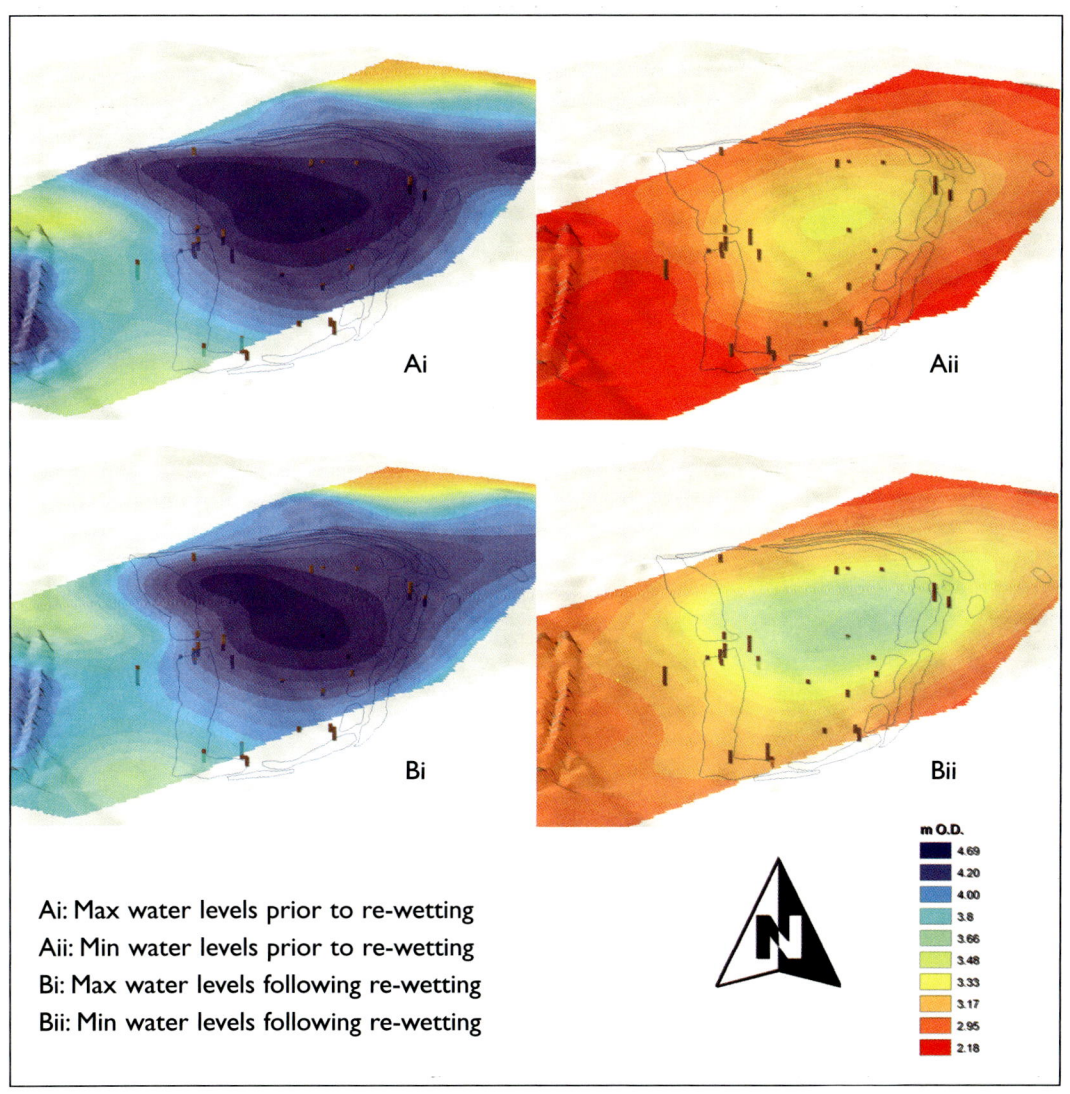

Ai: Max water levels prior to re-wetting
Aii: Min water levels prior to re-wetting
Bi: Max water levels following re-wetting
Bii: Min water levels following re-wetting

m O.D.
4.69
4.20
4.00
3.8
3.66
3.48
3.33
3.17
2.95
2.18

The position and depth of buried archaeological wood is shown in relation to the ground and ground water levels.

my steps for a short distance, I found the keys lying next to one of my piezometers. I had been very lucky, and Sutton Common had been merciful.

One of the aims of the monitoring programme was to understand the impact of the engineering work carried out to raise the level of the water table. This involved capturing the water flowing from the field drains which ran below the ground surface and also the installation of dams within the drainage ditches, both measures designed to prevent water from flowing from the site.

Changes were also occurring in the way that Sutton Common was being managed at this time. The vegetation was being changed to grass and cattle were being grazed by farmer Andrew Booth. Again making use of the capabilities of GIS, it was possible from excavation records going back to 1998, to create a database of the location of archaeological wood. This was then integrated with assessed surfaces representing the highest and lowest values for the water table for before and after the re-wetting. Essentially this was a process of comparison to identify any differences, and if these existed then to characterise them, therefore providing information to help measure the success of the re-wetting work.

This process resulted in integrated models of the archaeological wood and information on the water table viewed from a three-dimensional perspective. What can be seen is that the maximum recorded levels for the water table before re-wetting were very similar to those after. However, the minimum levels were different, with a higher recorded water table following the re-wetting. This suggested that there has been a positive impact on the water table.

So rewetting was working at keeping the water table a little higher, but this only makes sense when looked at in relation to the organic archaeology present on the site. From the exercise it was clear that the majority of the wood identified was subjected to at least intermittently dry conditions, unsuitable for its continued preservation. The amount that the water table was raised was not great enough to alter this situation, therefore the regrettable conclusion must be drawn that the reworking of the field drainage was insufficient to ensure the future preservation of the organic archaeological resource throughout the site.

From a scientific perspective, this conclusion is not as unhelpful as it might sound. The monitoring exercise achieved its primary goal of assessing the impact of the re-wetting work that was carried out. Now this is known, ways in which the situation can be improved further are being investigated, and this is a step towards a potentially successful outcome.

As mentioned previously, during the course of the monitoring programme, it became clear that the changes observed within the water table were influenced mainly by rainfall and through the level of water loss via vegetation (evapotranspiration) rather than field drainage.

A change which occurred at the same time as the physical changes to the field drainage was in the management of the site itself. Prior to the summer of 2000, little active management existed other than the topping of vegetation to inhibit thistle growth, (something that was not always very successful, as I learned to my cost).

During this time, the field was what could easily be termed 'wild' and it often showed in the plant and wildlife. I recall seeing leverets, owls, snakes and lizards during my monitoring visits along with numerous wild plants, and I especially remember the carpet of poppies that greeted the coming of summer. However, this was in essence a field that had been left to its own devices and was not sustainable.

With the diligent care of Andrew Booth, the site was once more transformed into a working piece of land, but where previously the archaeology had been subjected to the destructive influence of ploughing, cattle now roamed. This has possibly been of the greatest benefit to the water table, as the removal of the unmanaged vegetation also removed the major conduit for removal of water from below the ground surface, and this may explain the subsequent rise observed within the hydrological models.

However, cattle are not necessarily the archaeologist's best friend, and this change has compelled the development of monitoring equipment. I was once told to be wary of cows: "They're inquisitive creatures and

Cattle playing ball with a concrete block!

given the chance, they'll lick the paint off your car!" A bit of a myth, I thought!

Before the cattle were on Sutton Common, I located the piezometers by placing painted canes in the ground. I was used to getting on site and seeing these canes stretching off into the distance towards Shirley Wood. The first time I arrived with the cattle on, I was horrified to find that the canes were no longer there. So began a period of change in which I tried to outwit twenty cows, a challenge which I often failed! The problem seemed to be that the canes attracted the cows to the location of the piezometers, so not only were the canes themselves removed, but often the piezometers were trampled well into the ground making the taking of readings impossible.

Helped by Andrew, I tried a number of possible solutions including protecting the equipment by tyres and concrete blocks, but both were unsuccessful. Once I was greeted by seeing a cow toss a tyre into the air and chase after it, and another time by a number of them rolling a 20 kg concrete block down the site track! This latter occasion was also the time that I realised that the 'myth' had an element of truth to it when I nearly had a wing mirror licked off.

However, all was not doom and gloom. This experience has shown that to ensure successful, continued monitoring, it is essential that equipment is physically safeguarded, even if at the beginning there is seemingly no need for it. Future monitoring on Sutton Common will take this into account. I never did manage to monitor the site when the cows were there: Bovines 1 – Human 0!

In conclusion, the monitoring programme which was carried out on Sutton Common has been successful in achieving its primary aims. We now understand in great detail how the water table behaves from the network of piezometers, and also how this influences other factors within the burial environment, such as soil chemical conditions and microbiological activity.

We have also accurately assessed the impact of the re-wetting work on the water table and concluded that even though there has been an overall rise in the water table, it has not been sufficient to ensure the *in situ* preservation of the archaeological wood which still survives within the ground.

However, because we now understand in better detail why this situation exists, it is possible to set new aims and identify new means by which they can be achieved, including new ways to raise the water table in the future.

From an academic and scientific point of view, this has furthered our knowledge in this discipline and provided valuable experience that can be applied on other important wetland archaeological sites which require protection. This includes the techniques and approaches that were developed during the monitoring programme, such as the archaeological wood model, and the way in which information is presented. All these can be used in the future to form the basis for new research.

The data gathered can be used to predict where ground water would break the surface at different levels.

JAMES CHEETHAM

James has had an interest in wetland archaeology since childhood, having grown up on the fringes of Lindow Bog, Cheshire and well remembers the excitement caused by the discovery of Lindow man during the 1980s. He has been involved with Sutton Common since 1998, when he worked on the initial excavations carried out by the Centre for Wetland Archaeology. At this time, he was completing an MSc in wetland archaeological science and management following graduation with a BSc degree in physical geography, both at the University of Hull. Sponsored by the Carstairs Countryside Trust, James was offered the opportunity to undertake research in the monitoring of the site at Sutton Common towards his PhD, which he successfully obtained.

CHAPTER SEVEN

RAISING THE LEVELS

A waterlogged site is usually something a landowner wants to avoid. Not so in the case of Sutton Common, where new works to re-create wet conditions were required to save the archaeology, as **IAN CARSTAIRS** explains

Just because you own a piece of land and think you want to raise the water-levels, doesn't mean that you can just go out, block the ditches and drains and expect everything to be alright. Apart from anything else ... there can be a *right* kind of water and a *wrong* kind of water. And most importantly every landowner has a legal obligation not to do anything disadvantageous to the drainage of a neighbour's property.

Preparation for tackling the raising of the water table is an exacting task. But it proved a first-class exercise to test the reality of the concept that there can be 'Value in wetness' and to prove that economic farming, environmental benefits and social regeneration issues can be harmonised to the advantage of all.

Once the Centre for Wetland Archaeology had undertaken surveys to map the topography, assess the relative state of preservation, determine the sub-surface water table levels and their fluctuations throughout the year and subsequently identify the optimum height for the water table which could deliver *in situ* preservation of organic remains, CCT's trustees moved on to address how this might be achieved.

The studies carried out by CWA suggested that the target level to achieve sufficient wetness would be some 4.1m above sea level in the ditches of the small enclosure. A preliminary judgment had already been taken that we could not achieve levels relative to the position of buried archaeological deposits similar to that which prevailed prior to mining subsidence and the implementation of various drainage works. To have done so would have required a level resulting in a lake stretching from Doncaster to the Humber Estuary – a veritable Lake Humber II.

Also the condition of the deposits varied between those which potentially could be preserved, those which were marginal, and those which would not survive our lifetimes. On the latter, it would turn out that we were much closer to the line of its disappearance than we

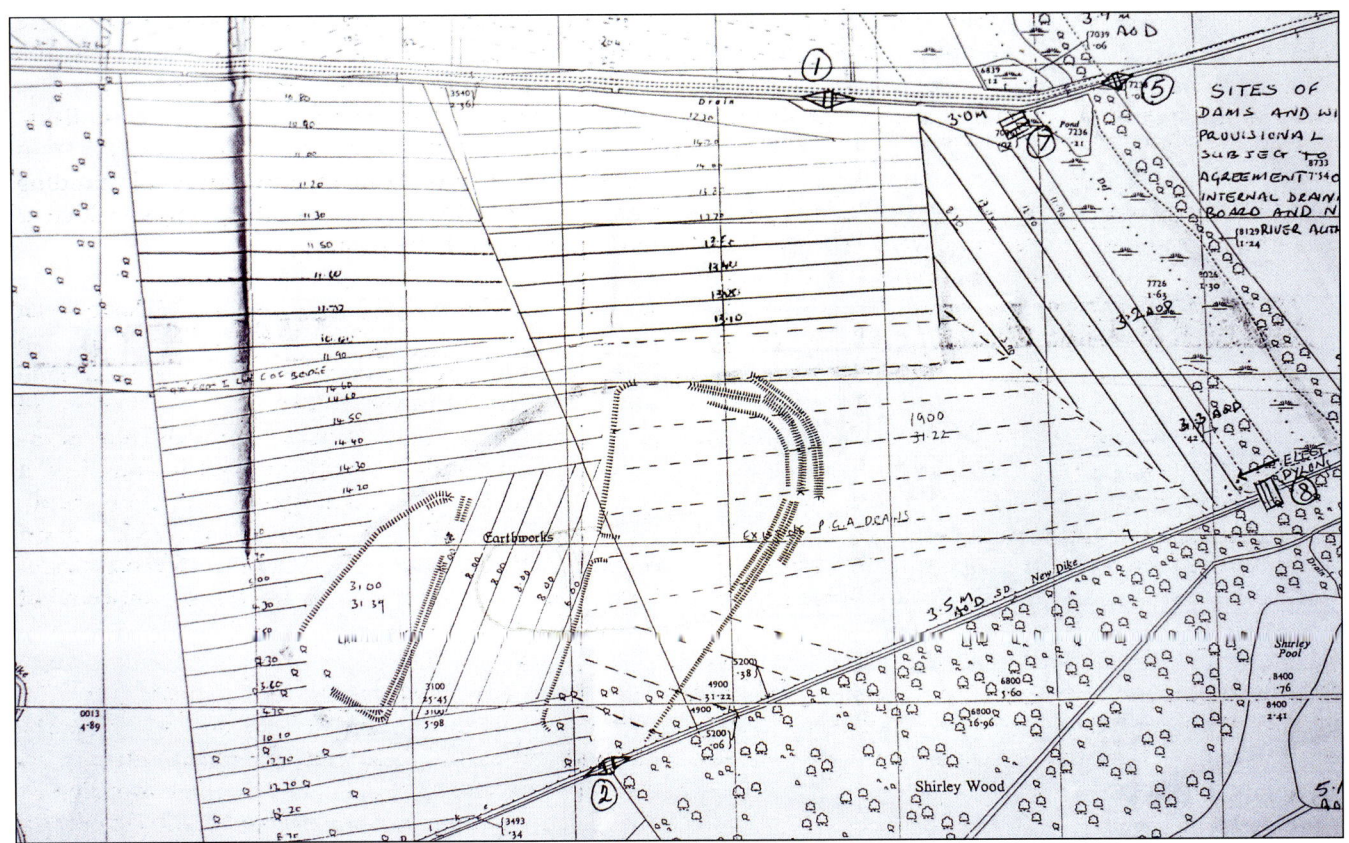

A plan of the extensive agricultural under-field drains installed on Sutton Common.

RE-WETTING

Re-wetting makes the groundwater level rise and this leads to improved preservation of archaeological remains, such as those at Sutton Common which have not been excavated. The concept of re-wetting is still very new, and the study of its effects on the soil and the organic remains is of considerable scientific importance.

imagined at this time. However, research had shown that the water table is not flat but domed under the Scheduled Ancient Monument, and this gave some leeway for the target level at the banks of the drains to be consequently lower.

To tackle the problem, consulting drainage engineers Grantham Brundell and Farran were commissioned to provide an engineering options study for water-level control. The brief required GBF to address how the desired levels of ground water could be achieved in three different ways, namely:

- contained within Sutton Common and with no impact on surrounding land;
- contained within Sutton Common and Shirley Pool combined; and
- unconstrained in order to see what the impact (if any) would be and how far any effects would extend.

Consideration of the three approaches included details of engineering works, consents and licences required, and legal requirement for pursuing the chosen course of action.

Fortuitously, the feasibility study had a head-start, since GBF had already recently conducted a significant range of relevant research for English Nature concerning water quality and quantity in the neighbouring Shirley Pool Site of Special Scientific Interest (SSSI).

Hydrologically, the site and surrounding lands lie in the base of a depression in the land – in effect a sump – which was extremely good news. Being at the lowest point of the immediate water-catchment reduced the potential problems of lateral impact – i.e. flooding – from raised water levels on surrounding land.

Next the character of the soils was considered. These change from peats in the east of the site to mineral soils and clays to the west, crossed by the peaty course of the prehistoric river channel of the Hampole Beck. In wet conditions this transition can be readily seen in aerial photographs, both by the extent of standing water and also by the colour of the grass which is darker green over the peat.

In the past, the natural drainage would have been from the Common out through Shirley Pool. In recent years however, artificial works to ameliorate the impact of coal-mining subsidence and laying of agricultural field drains to improve production intercepted that natural flow and directed it away into a rigid pattern of deep drainage ditches. As a result, both the Scheduled Ancient Monument with its buried organic archaeological remains and the fen habitats of Shirley Pool and their wildlife have been deprived of the water which they required.

Critical to any judgements to be made was the assimilation of the recorded land and water levels. Most reliance was placed on the recent surveys, as these were relatively unaffected by land movements due to coal-mining subsidence and peat shrinkage. However, to give as complete a picture as possible over a large area and time-span, other research undertaken by GBF, South Yorkshire Archaeology and the Dun Drainage Commissioners was also considered as the back-cloth to assessing relative levels.

Most important to the progress of any project involving the manipulation of water, and vital to be considered at the earliest stage, are the legal constraints placed on a landowner when it involves changes to water levels. These obligations derive particularly from Land Drainage Acts, under which it is an offence to reduce the efficiency of drainage of another persons

Rex Carson and Bruce Keith of English Nature struggle out of a deep ditch created to improve drainage.

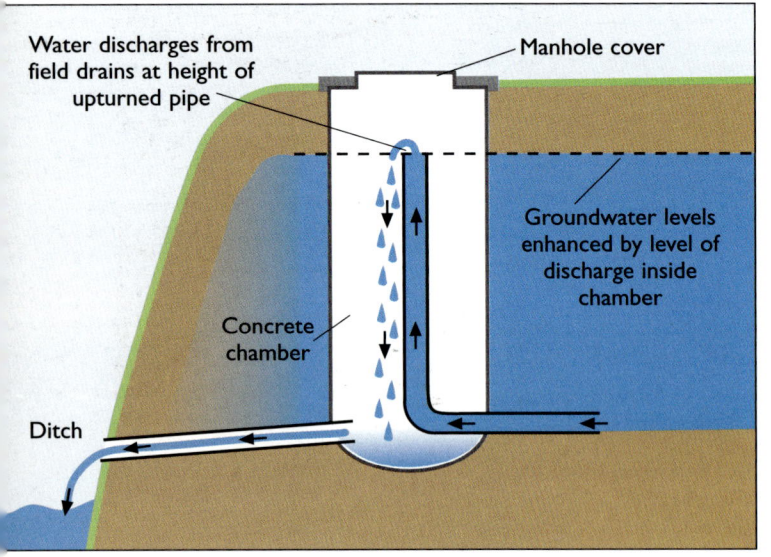

Water discharges from field drains at height of upturned pipe

Manhole cover

Groundwater levels enhanced by level of discharge inside chamber

Concrete chamber

Ditch

A re-engineered drain outfall – how it works.

property; and water resources, reservoirs, Ancient Monument and Wildlife and Countryside legislation. In any proposed works, many consents would be necessary. In addition, the routes of overhead electricity supply and communications lines, a government oil pipeline, and telephone cables as well as water supply pipes needed to be taken into consideration.

The CWA surveys revealed that the ground levels at Sutton Common range from 2.9m to 5.2m above sea level. The target level for groundwater at the ditches of the small enclosure had been defined, as stated above, bearing in mind the condition of buried remains and their location relative in the soil strata.

Simply containing and rewetting within CCT's land holding had distinct advantages, not least that it could be tackled without the complications of negotiations with third-parties. It was also particularly reassuring that the study showed that the desired outcome might be achieved relatively easily without any likely adverse impact on neighbouring property.

Managing the Common in a co-ordinated way with Shirley Pool, owned by John Steadman, a sympathetic neighbour, was also considered practical at very little extra cost. Indeed it would have been blinkered in the extreme not to plan to combine the two, as it soon became clear that without taking the two together, once the water was raised on Sutton Common, it could well simply run out of the back-door through Shirley Pool and round into the main drains. It also became clear that to carry this work out to best effect, CCT needed to own another block of land, Rushy Moor, to the north, which it subsequently successfully bought. Ownership of this extra parcel of land freed the Trust to install the full suite of engineering works required to stop the water running out in a different direction.

The proposals put forward by GBF were imaginative and relatively easy and cheap to implement. To the uninitiated, it might be tempting to think that all you needed to do was to block the ends of the field under-drains and that would hold the water back. Of course it might for a short while, but with permeable pipes running to the outfall and a head of water building, the pressure near the pipe-end would sooner or later force the water out and burst the ditch banks.

To overcome this in a sustainable way, the permeable drain pipes were lifted several metres back from their outfall. These were then replaced with impermeable pipes, such that the water could not readily leak out into the surrounding soil near the ditches. These pipes were then linked into concrete chambers spaced around the common. Once inside the chambers, the pipes were turned upwards so as to discharge at a level set by the number of sections in the up-turned pipe, the resultant height of the water table outside the chamber. The draining water then fell back down inside the concrete chamber to discharge at the same level as previously into the ditches.

The underdrains were therefore not destroyed, simply re-engineered. Two dams were then placed in lateral drains and these also held back water from running out of Shirley Pool.

Once the alterations to the drains on Sutton Common had been completed, it had been intended to carry out the same exercise on those at Rushy Moor to stop water seeping across and into a main drain running south-north bisecting this extra land. However, under close inspection, the under-drains were found to be blocked with debris and not functioning. So they were simply left alone, lest by disturbing them they started to drain where no draining was actually taking place –

A new impermeable pipe is laid.

Constructing a discharge chamber.

and incidentally saving more than eight thousand pounds into the bargain.

For completeness, the unconstrained approach to delivering levels of 4.1m above sea level was tested although it had been obvious from the outset that to try to deliver that full level in such a flat landscape, if it had been possible, would have had an impact well beyond the limits of the land owned by the Trust. Naturally this option was not seriously considered, but illustrated well why you can't just block the drains and get on with it.

To date, the raised levels have had a significant impact on groundwater levels, but more of the right sort of water is still needed. As James Cheetham described (in Chapter 6), it simply does not rain enough to hold the levels throughout the year, and the need to supplement the supply in some way is a real future consideration.

But even that is not simple, for the type of water required for Shirley Pool is not the same as that for Sutton Common. The former depends an oxygenated supply of gently-moving alkaline water to sustain the habitat, while the latter, with its buried organic remains, would prefer a reservoir of static, stinking, stagnant, oxygen-deficient water permeating the ground. More interesting work still lies ahead.

CHAPTER EIGHT

FEEDING THE FEN

Rewetting is also the buzz word in the conservation of important wetland wildlife sites. Here English Nature's **TIM KOHLER** explains how the work at Sutton Common, while assisting the preservation of the archaeology, is also helping to keep Shirley Pool an oasis for wildlife.

Close to Sutton Common is a protected wildlife area and Site of Special Scientific Interest (SSSI) known as Shirley Pool. This long strip of wet woodland and fen surrounding a still pool is all that remains of the wildlife habitat which would have dominated the scene before the enclosures were made. It almost certainly represents a near miraculous survival of the 'wood-pasture' recorded in this area in the Domesday Book over nine hundred years ago.

Lying in what is thought to be one of the old river channels or possibly an abandoned peat-digging, it is a mysterious place, almost a little bit of landscape that time forgot. Standing well back from roads and closely watched over by the shooting syndicate to which it is let by its owner, it experiences little disturbance.

The wetter areas are mostly sedge marsh, made up of great fen sedge, and an open expanse of almost head-high tussocks of large, stiff-leaved sedge with dangerously-sharp, saw-edged leaves. But they also include among others two delightfully-cheerful and showy spring plants, flag iris and marsh marigold. Some of the other wet open areas are dominated by the feathery heads of common reed, the fat brown sausages of reed-mace (often called bulrush) and a range of other sedges and rushes.

At the heart of this oasis for wildife lies the substantial pool from which the site takes its name, and alongside that, willow carr and very wet woodland, with the willows and alders growing on waterlogged soil. In summer, the grass snake, Britain's largest and an excellent swimmer, is sometimes spotted in the pool or in the drains leading across the common.

This damp and sheltered area is good for mosses and ferns, including the rare marsh fern. On the slightly

Greater pond sedge.

Yellow flag iris.

Shirley Pool from the air.

Willows fringe Shirley Pool.

higher and drier ground, the tree species change to birch and oak, and interspersed with all the other habitats there are also a few areas of wet grassland. It is quite a mixture for such a relatively small area.

Important places for wildlife are usually recognised for the type of habitat and the important species they hold. Although not formally recognised for its birds, Shirley Pool does form an important refuge for a range of relatively common species, providing both roosting sites and food in the form of insects and seeds. Flocks of tits, including long tailed-tit and willow tit, are fairly common in the winter, some of which breed here in the summer. Reed bunting and sedge warbler are other notable residents.

Wading birds, such as curlew and greenshank, have been recorded from the area in the past, and it is hoped that these types of birds will return more frequently as the surrounding land is returned to damp grassland. Indeed, curlew have been seen regularly in the spring, along with large numbers of skylarks, and both now nest on Sutton Common.

TRIPLE SIs

Sites of Special Scientific Interest (SSSI) are designated by English Nature, the government's wildlife advisors. The sites are selected for their important wildlife value, and although mainly privately owned, the designation protects the sites from actions which would damage their wildlife interest. In compensation for these restrictions, English Nature is able to pay grants to owners to assist with the management of the sites for wildlife.

Heron.

Young tawny owl.

Kestrels and barn owls haunt the grassland in search of food, and in one winter, three short-eared owls stayed for several weeks, hunting through the fen and out over the open, misty, low-lit Common. Herons often visit the ditches, and good numbers of the increasingly-scarce grey partridge and hares both make use of cover on the drier edge of the fen. The delicate roe deer, one of Britain's only two native species of deer (the other is the red), are also frequently seen.

Plants and birds are perhaps the most obvious wildlife because they are so easily seen. But look a little closer and we find a large range of insects, some of which are at the very northern limits of their range. One of these is the hairy dragonfly, unsurprisingly given its name, the hairiest of Britain's dragonflies, and known from nowhere else in Yorkshire.

Many insects are much less visible (and much harder to find) such as the soldier beetle, which has the scientific name of *Silus ruficollis* and which runs around among the stems of the reeds catching smaller insects. This is known only from Shirley Pool in the whole of northern England. Another very obvious insect is a rather vicious horsefly; its bite is extremely unpleasant but on the up-side, it does have beautiful iridescent green eyes!

The water which feeds the pool is of particular importance, as it comes from a series of springs rising at the edge of the limestone ridge running north-south through Askern. With a concentration of dissolved minerals, the presence of this water results in soils much richer and more alkaline than most fens – the strong growth of the fen sedge being a clear sign. Since the plants depend directly on not only the right quantity but the right quality of water, it is vital to wildlife that this balance of water chemistry is maintained.

Large-scale drainage of much of the local area in medieval and later times means that there are very few wetland sites left – Shirley Pool is perhaps the best example of this type of fen remaining in the whole of South Yorkshire. But its recent past and both short and long-term future have been precarious, and its survival with a full range of species cannot be taken for granted.

Securing its future has not been for want of trying. English Nature and its predecessors have been involved directly in the site since the 1950s. First given legal protection as a Site of Special Scientific Interest (SSSI) in 1955, this was updated in 1983, when the site was notified under the current Wildlife and Countryside Act (1981).

At about the same time as English Nature carried out the review as part of its notification procedure, drainage issues took a turn for the worse. Subsidence due to coal mining had caused difficulties with the existing drainage pattern, and there was also strong pressure to improve the adjacent land – Sutton Common – for agriculture.

In practice, this meant yet more and better drainage of the land to the potential benefit of crop production, and for flood alleviation – but with serious consequences for wildlife. The story is a familiar one. The responsibility for drainage in this area lies with the Dun Drainage Commission. In response to these pressures and issues, the Commissioners proposed a scheme to deepen ditches, potentially seriously exacerbating the damage that adjacent drains were already causing.

The main drains ran through the middle of Shirley Pool and out into Stream Dyke at the north end by Rushy Moor Plantation. Deepening these ditches

FENLANDS

The peatlands surviving to the east of Sutton Common, around Rushy Moor and the Shirley Pool SSSI, receive plenty of nutrients from the rainwater which washes into the wetlands from the surrounding arable lands, and possibly also from an aquifer that feeds from below. The vegetation of this peatland is very different from the raised mires of the Thorne and Hatfield Moors because of its nutrient-rich character, and is known as a fen.

would have caused even more rapid drying-out, and an almost certain loss of much of its wildlife interest.

So back in the early 1980s, we agreed with the Dun Drainage Commissioners to modify that original idea. A new scheme was developed which involved re-routing the main drainage system by creating a new ditch further to the west. We knew there were likely to be some consequential problems with this, so together with the Commissioners, we tried to secure the boundaries, with a number of small weirs constructed across a number of old ditches in an attempt to hold water within the site.

Throughout the 1980s and the early 1990s, this new drainage system and the condition of Shirley Pool were monitored. Gradually it became clear that there remained a fundamental problem: like Sutton Common, it quite simply was still gradually drying out.

The various structures, including the original dams and weirs installed in the old ditches, were deteriorating,

Scrub tree-growth encroaches on the fen.

and some had started leaking. As the fen dried up, so the vegetation changed, the most obvious sign being the gradual development of trees and scrub, which could now flourish where formerly it had been too wet. Once established, the trees accelerated the drying process, drawing water up out of the ground through their roots and into their leaves, from where it was evaporating off into the air.

We needed imagination and urgent action to address this situation. Clearly, the obvious question was, how were we going to get water back into the SSSI to restore and retain the water levels? There were two main issues to consider: firstly, Shirley Pool had largely been cut off from its original supply of water, and secondly, the development of 'inappropriate' vegetation, which now was fuelling a self-perpetuating cycle of water loss – the more and bigger the trees, the worse the situation would become.

Dealing with the vegetation was perhaps the easiest part of the problem to answer. Through better manage-

ment, reducing the amount of shrub and tree growth, the water loss could be slowed. Working with John Steadman, who owns most of the protected site (the trustees of the Carstairs Conservation Trust own the rest), a programme of beneficial management was agreed through a Wildlife Enhancement Scheme grant.

Dealing with the lack of water proved more difficult, and it is at this point we started to make connections with the archaeological needs at Sutton Common. For both areas, the key to maintaining their respective interests is keeping them wet, but the difference in levels and variations in water chemistry required for each makes a combined scheme a testing proposition.

However, the less intensive grassland management of the Common next to Shirley Pool is expected to have significant wildlife benefits, providing additional feeding space particularly for the birds found on the site. It has also been noticed that the area of fen vegetation is beginning to spread out into the lower lying eastern ends of Rushy Moor, with plants like ragged robin appearing in the new grassland which were formerly under arable cropping.

Following various suggested solutions to the water supply problems, a trial was carried out in summer 1996 with the assistance of the Dun Drainage Commissioners, to test how the habitats would react to having water pumped onto it. While this may seem a rather obvious thing to do, the water movement below the ground surface in this area is complex, with many layers of interconnecting peat and sand separated by layers of clay. No one could predict with any certainty exactly what would happen to the water which was pumped on; although the site had been wet in the past, many changes have occurred to the drainage pattern and land and water levels in the soils over the last 20 years.

Ragged robin.

Stream dyke – a potential water supply for the fen.

The aim of the trial was first and foremost to see if we could retain water, or at least to find out whether the water would be lost through sub-surface (groundwater) or surface flows. But the water pumped on needed to be the right quality. Fortunately we have a good source of water in Stream Dike, running across the north of Rushy Moor and Shirley Pool, which is fed by springs from the original source which fed the site.

A temporary dam placed in the stream coupled with a mobile pump lifting water out of the dike enabled a steady supply to be pumped more than half a kilometre to the centre of the fen area. As pumping continued, the water in the soils was monitored until, after a week, the levels reached their upper limit where the pumping ceased to have any further effect. Slightly to our surprise, the water levels held up quite well, with a 'dome' of water building around the pumping discharge point which then spread out and gradually leaked away. This proved the basic concept, but still left us to deal with the vexed question as to how we would devise a long-term method for lifting water a metre or two and delivering it to the middle of the site.

Placing a diesel pump on Stream Dyke wasn't exactly a very environmentally nor economically-sustainable solution, requiring a constant input of effort and almost daily checks. An electric pump would be much simpler to operate, but there was no electricity supply, and it would be much too expensive to install.

A wind-pump was also considered; although this would have a lower capacity, it could operate over a longer period and would be much cheaper to main-

tain. Though quite vulnerable to vandalism, it may well prove to be the simplest answer in the long run, and an idea to which we will return following the developments on the Common. It also fits nicely with the environmental ethos of the overall scheme.

So, this brings us about up-to-date. The works undertaken to conserve the archaeology will secure one edge of Shirley Pool SSSI, and may yet provide a small amount of water to enhance the levels. More importantly, they are helping to stem the loss of water in a westerly direction. The second group of works to improve the dams and water retaining structures, especially at the north end, will hopefully make a further and more noticeable difference to the wetness of Shirley Pool, but, as with the water needs of the Common itself, further measures may still be necessary. These can only be delivered through a continued partnership with CCT, the Dun Drainage Commission, and the owner of Shirley Pool, if the wildlife is to be maintained and flourish into the future.

One of the new dams on Sutton Common which help to retain water in Shirley Pool.

The exploded seed head of reed mace.

TIM KOHLER

Tim graduated from Wolverhampton Polytechnic with an applied biology degree in 1986. He worked with wildlife trusts in Wales and the Border before joining the Nature Conservancy Council in 1990 as an assistant conservation officer covering the West Midlands. He later became a Regional Urban Officer covering Essex, Suffolk, Norfolk and Hertfordshire. He took up the post of Conservation Officer for South Yorkshire in May 1992, where his responsibilities involved overseeing Sites of Special Scientific Interest, including Shirley Pool near Sutton Common. After a spell concentrating on biodiversity issues, encouraging and assisting with the development of Local Biodiversity Action Plans, he now deals with Thorne and Hatfield Moors.

CHAPTER NINE

VALUE IN WETNESS

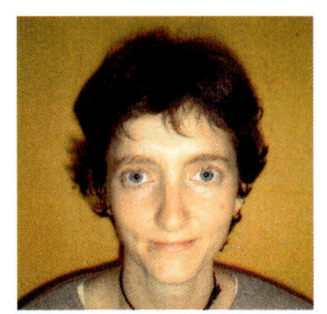

At an early stage in the Sutton Common saga, vital help was offered by the Government's countryside agencies. **STUART PASLEY** and **VIV CHEETHAM** describe how the rules have been used to advantage to help shape what might become a blueprint for the future of water and land management.

In 1998, not long after the Carstairs Conservation Trust (CCT) bought Sutton Common, the trustees approached the Ministry of Agriculture Fisheries and Food (MAFF) – as Defra (Department for the Environment, Food and Rural Affairs) was then known – with an application to join the Countryside Stewardship Scheme.

This scheme, often known in farming and nature conservation circles simply as 'Stewardship', provides a range of financial support aimed at encouraging less intensive and environmentally beneficial ways of farming. With a major task ahead of them to revert some 70 acres/28ha from the weedy mess of set-aside to a wet grassland (subsequently a further 65 acres/26ha of Rushy Moor were added) the Trust needed all the help it could get.

The trustees of CCT had always been keen to point out that while their aims are to deliver environmental

benefits, the scope to do this depended on economically-sound farming to deliver the land management and habitat development desired. This was especially important as the Trust, working with the Sutton Common Group, had an ambitious set of aims for the land.

It was clear from the outset that this would be no ordinary Stewardship Scheme. To start with the rules forbid ploughing, spraying or digging up in any way the grass once it has been established. Yet regularly letters arrived at the Stewardship office requesting permission to do something unusual – often involving excavation of quite large areas of the site – though there were always the very best of reasons for doing it. On each occasion, express consent to vary the agreement had to be sought from Defra.

The trustees willingly accepted that though we knew their aims to be good and true, they still needed to

What is the Countryside Stewardship Scheme? It is:

- Set up in 1992, it is one of the Government's schemes for improving the countryside
- Under it, landowners/managers enter into ten-year agreements to carry out works benefiting the landscape, wildlife, historical features and public enjoyment of the countryside.
- There are now approximately 12,000 schemes countrywide.

Hay bales in fen meadows.

Mowing thistles.

jump through all the hoops and do everything by the book. And it wasn't just digging up the grass that needed consent either. There were issues like our friends the thistles, which exacted such a toll on James Cheetham's knees, and too many cows here and not enough there, which posed repeated problems.

Now thistles in moderation can be a good thing for wildlife, such as for bees and butterflies and for 'charms' of seed-eating birds such as goldfinches. But

acres of them is a completely different matter. Even with regular grazing, the sea of thistles was overwhelming the grassland.

After a botanical survey of the site by a Defra ecologist to ensure no vegetation of value would be damaged, it was agreed to spray the whole field with a herbicide to kill off the thistles, hopefully once and for all. Duly completed, it made an enormous difference, giving a chance to get on top of the problem, at least for a while.

Grazing levels also required exceptions to be made. Stewardship agreements normally stipulate low stocking in spring and early summer to reduce disturbance to ground-nesting birds such as the skylark, and to allow more grasses and flowers to set seed without being nibbled-off.

In the years of the excavations, before the digging commenced, higher grazing levels on the common had to be approved so no stock would be present while the digging was underway (the cows may have been interested, as we have already heard from James

Cheetham, but perhaps not too helpful). It was also important to get the vegetation short, otherwise the grass would end up far too long by the end of the season. The cattle then had to be moved onto Rushy Moor – which meant that site exceeded the agreed stocking rate….and so it went on.

It was a constant juggling act, each time with a consent procedure to be followed, and paper to be processed. But the flexible approach was absolutely vital and the results more than justified the effort.

The value of the Stewardship funding to CCT cannot be over-estimated: it allowed a more sustainable future for Sutton Common and Rushy Moor to be developed. Most importantly, the income gave the Trust the capacity to participate as a catalyst for wider research to test how similar things could be achieved on other land.

The timing was perfect. At the critical early stages of work on Sutton Common, great debates were raging over extremes of floods on one hand and summer water shortages and continuing loss of wetlands on the other. Against this backdrop, the attention of decision-makers was turning to the idea that there might be a better way of looking at water, rather than just rushing it as fast as possible to the sea, only to shortly after-wards lament that there was not enough to go around.

We were beginning to look in earnest at new ways of managing this valuable resource to see whether it could be linked to much wider public and private benefits. The Humberhead Levels Land Management Initiative was our response to exploring the problems and opportunities.

At the time, the potential work to be carried out here made Sutton Common a 'natural' for exploring some

Impenetrable vegetation.

Low intensity grazing benefits nesting birds.

of the ideas behind 'Value in Wetness', the name given to the initiative's research programme. In effect, it provided a real-world kick-start and an immediate and tangible expression to the purposes of the Humberhead Levels scheme. More especially, Sutton Common formed the perfect focus for research connected with raising water levels, as well as a convenient testing ground to investigate the realities of farming within Stewardship to deliver integrated economic, social and environmental benefits.

With such a golden opportunity, it was no surprise that it soon became the first pilot project in the scheme which has now developed into providing a major contribution to influencing the way we think in this country about water and land management.

The Lower Derwent Valley – winter floods naturally fertilise the ancient flood-plain meadows.

But to return to the Value in Wetness programme and Sutton Common's role in it. We firstly need to take a geographical step back, to consider a larger area where Sutton Common is placed into a broader setting. Secondly, we need to move away from practical concerns – the way Countryside Stewardship is helping to manage the site – to think about how our experiences are contributing to the development of regional, national and even European agricultural and rural development policies.

The Humberhead Levels is an area with a fascinating history, much of it closely related to water and water management. Ever since the drainage attempts by Cornelius Vermuyden in the seventeenth century and latterly via the Internal Drainage Boards (IDBs), Man has reclaimed the wetlands for the benefit of agriculture and the people who live there. Once drained, the silted-up former lake bed we see today has provided us with one of the most fertile agricultural areas in England, but there are still a number of issues relating to water and land management which need to be addressed.

Some of the area is below sea level, so there is a need to protect against floods as well as to dry the land sufficiently to allow arable cropping. Water is taken out of the area either from the sandstone aquifer which underlies parts of it, or from the rivers which are flowing through it, for the use of industry, for people and, just a little bit, for agriculture. In some cases the soils get too dry for crops to grow in the summer, requiring irrigation in order to provide the water when it is needed. Plus, of course, there are wetland-biodiversity issues in terms of wetland wildlife habitats at sites such as Shirley Pool; and in wetland archaeology, with places such as Sutton Common drying-out to the point where their heritage value is seriously threatened.

Rich arable lands stretch between Thorne Moors and the River Ouse.

VALUE IN WETNESS

The key objectives in the Value in Wetness Initiative are:-

- Pursuing integrated economic, social and environmental aims for sustainable water and land manage ment in arable areas;
- Providing proof that alternative management of water could bring environmental, social and economic benefits;
- Setting out practical methods of achieving the defined objectives, including small site demonstrations, and practical ways of implementing the EU Water Frameworks Directive;
- Making recommendations concerning the changes required to other policies to assist and add value to implementation of the Directive;
- Making an analysis of the potential for the Internal Drainage Boards to have a broader and more positive role in water management.

Attractive riverscapes are a magnet for tourism.

The "Value in Wetness" initiative is co-ordinated by a partnership of organisations including English Nature; English Heritage; the Environment Agency; Grantham, Brundell and Farran, (representing the Internal Drainage Boards), and the Countryside Agency. Each brings their own particular expertise and objectives, but all are working together to achieve a greater whole.

Trying to balance all these different demands is a considerable task, and policies have not yet come close to cracking it. And that's what we are now attempting to do through Value in Wetness by seeking new, economically viable, environmentally sensitive approaches to water and land management. Hopefully some real things are happening on some real sites – such as at Sutton Common – but the main activity is about learning lessons, so that we can try to influence policy development.

Vital to any success has been the need for clear and relevant information. To this end, nine pilot sites were identified. Sutton Common was the first, and is certainly the one where most has been happening. That's largely because of the wide partnership of organisations that have been able to contribute expertise and money to the work and through CCT assessing, experimenting with and adjusting management in a sort of game of three-dimensional environmental chess. It was still a very steep learning curve for everyone, though.

Value in Wetness has an interest in the detailed archaeology, but it is not our main reason for being involved. English Heritage and the universities

Traditional haymaking in an SSSI.

Below: *Too much water in winter – the River Don on the brink near the redundant Thorpe Marsh Power Station.*

provide this expertise. We have an interest in the biodiversity-value, but again, it is not our main reason for being involved; that is English Nature's remit. What we are interested in are the things we can learn from the way the site is being managed and the implications this holds for the way that other similar sites might be managed – and, therefore, how policies need to be shaped for the future.

Beyond the direct work at Sutton Common, the site has been a focus for the Royal Holloway Institute for Environmental Research in its efforts to define more precisely the wider benefits which can be achieved. Although management of water for agriculture through drainage and irrigation is an important consideration, it is only a very small part of the story.

For example, in the case of Sutton Common, the primary objective of the water management is to preserve the buried archaeology. Equally, somewhere else water might be managed to avoid flooding or perhaps for recreation as part of a leisure or tourism-related enterprise. There are many different reasons for managing water; sometimes they can be carried out in harmony, in others there may be direct conflicts. So, a part of the process has been to go back to basics and to challenge assumptions and received wisdom.

A further important piece of research, this time by Posford Haskoning, consultants with water and land management expertise, involved investigating different options and ways that useful advice can be offered to farmers and land managers to help them balance the different demands on water use, and subsequently to make the most of the opportunities open to them. An on-farm advisory package, called 'Positive Water Management', has been developed which will provide useful material for farmers to use as part of their farm-business planning.

While the land holding here at Sutton Common might have been under the control of a sympathetic conservation trust, we all knew that success in the broadest sense as an example to others was not about being starry-eyed over archaeology and wildlife, but could only be claimed if the operation never lost sight of the facts of down-to-earth economic farming reality. If it did, there would be no validity in the achievements, and the practical examples it might set to others to carry out similar imaginative schemes on their land would not amount to very much.

That is why, alongside the conservation work, a hard-nosed economic study was undertaken by Neville Turton, rural adviser, and Carter Jonas. This looked at the potential income from the land in arable production as at the time of purchase and then again

Harvest in the Humberhead Levels.

as the wet grassland to which the land had reverted. It not only explored the relative incomes of cropping and farming – in hand, contracted or let – but also, with the assistance of the District Valuer, it investigated the effects of works and land use change on the capital value of the land over the research period.

But what has been the implication of this change in terms of profitability? All very well for a trust with conservation objectives to be managing a site, but if it was a farmer who owned Sutton Common, could he afford to put the land into this kind of management or would it be losing money for the farm business?

The conclusions we arrived at were largely quite positive. Some engineering works to deal with the particular archaeological problem were needed, which incurred some expensive. But even allowing for the capital costs, it does seem that such a scheme could be a practical proposition for other land managers,

100

subject to one thing: that the farmer had a stock enterprise, or could let it to someone who did, or could make profitable use of a large amount of grass.

It is an inescapable fact that each generation tends to accept the world as they find it and see it in their lifetimes. But it is also important to remember that the whole landscape of England has undergone substantial and continuous change throughout history and prehistory. Understanding this change provides pointers to management needs in the future.

To make this easier to appreciate, a further project has been visualising the past, present and possible future appearance of Sutton Common. Produced through an experimental computer presentation developed by the Universities of East Anglia and Hull, it harnesses elaborate techniques to show the retreat of the ice; the Stone Age; the Bronze Age; the Iron Age; and today, together with a projection of our work into the future. With these images, it becomes much easier to see that nothing stands still, whether by forces of nature wholly independent of people, or by the actions of human kind itself.

But what does all this complex range of cutting-edge work achieve? At the outset, in true pioneering fashion, we had no real idea where it would lead us. If the way was clear and we'd known exactly what we were doing and where we were going, there would have been no point in doing anything at all. From this consistent and sustained effort over the last five years we do believe there is real scope to influence policy over water management issues in four key areas, namely:

- the Government's review of the England Rural Development Plan – the way a substantial amount of European money is delivered to rural England;
- the Government's Strategy for Sustainable Farming and Food and Farming 'Framework for Change' which has identified the Humberhead Levels as a priority for action, building on the work of the Value in Wetness Initiative;
- future reforms of the Common Agricultural Policy – the source of large amounts of money for the agricultural community; and finally
- the European Union Water Framework Directive, governing fundamental rules about the way water will be managed in the future.

A group of influential specialists learn about the achievements at Sutton Common.

All dry and very dusty stuff, you might say, and a world away from the excitement of touching the axe-marks on 2000-year-old timbers or relaxing on a lazy early summer's afternoon to the buzz of insects and the splendour of marsh plants. Many of these things have been lost in the past because land and water use was in conflict with their needs, as farmers strove to deliver the food society demanded.

So, dry though the talk of national and European policies may seem, these are nevertheless the vital tools at the heart of forging a new harmony between different needs, if wetland sites are not to continue to dry out and wither to dust themselves. Through these policies lies the route to success. Without them heading in the right direction, it will be an uphill – or perhaps we should we say an upstream – struggle.

Sutton Common itself has come a very long way back from the brink of total loss, but its future is not quite wholly secure yet. However, through imagination and co-operation it is showing that solutions to these highly complex problems can be found, if you just take them in 'salami slices'; each one thin enough to cope with at the time, but every one moving the whole process a step nearer success.

STUART PASLEY

Stuart is a Senior Countryside Officer with the Countryside Agency in Yorkshire and the Humber Region, where he leads regional policy work on rural economies, agriculture and land management, sustainable local products and tourism and regional delivery work including the 'Eat The View' programme, two Land Management Initiatives (LMIs) and the promotion of sustainable tourism. He manages the Countryside Agency's Humberhead Levels Land Management Initiative, known locally as Value in Wetness, which is seeking new, economically viable and environmentally sensitive approaches to water and land management, as a contribution to the national and European debate about reform of the Common Agriculture Policy and the development of wider, rural development policies.

VIV CHEETHAM

Viv grew up on a dairy farm in Cheshire, and graduated from Hull University in 1993 with a BA Hons in social policy and criminology. She then spent three years involved with charitable organisations such as the Scottish Wildlife and Groundwork Trusts, carrying out various practical conservation tasks. She also completed a post-graduate diploma at Manchester Metropolitan University in countryside management. In 1997, Viv joined the then Farming & Rural Conservation Agency (now the Rural Development Service, part of Defra) to work on the Countryside Stewardship Scheme where she now covers cases in South Yorkshire.

CHAPTER TEN

THE PAST BECOMES THE FUTURE

The involvement of the local community has been a vital ingredient in the success of the Sutton Common project. Here, **HOWARD CONNELL** of the North Doncaster Rural Trust explains how he become involved – and his ambitious plans for the future

Nearly forty years ago, I was a young student teacher supplementing my college grant by working in the summer holidays driving a Mr Softee ice cream van. On one memorable day in August 1967, I was sent to sell ice cream on the streets of Askern. The overcast, miserable day did nothing to help, but I was totally unprepared for the vision that awaited me.

I had passed through Askern on the A19 in a car as a child and cast envious glances towards the lake, where there always seemed to be children on the boats enjoying themselves. How I had wished that we had a boating lake close to my home in Woodlands so that I too could have gone and enjoyed myself boating at the weekend, as the children in Askern evidently did.

As I arrived in Askern, I had a vision of that attractive lake firmly implanted in my mind and so was ill-prepared for the reality of the back streets. On that wet August day, I turned into the Instoneville mining

Askern Lake from the air.

Aerial view of the Coalite Works – now closed and demolished.

The Coalite Works dominate the town.

Sutton Common is in the distance in this view from the Coalite Works.

estate, and had my first introduction to the Askern Coalite Coking Plant. As I drove around the streets there was an acrid smell that somehow found the back of my throat. Smoke hung everywhere, and the sight of the plant in operation with the attendant noise, smells and flames was very alarming to someone unaccustomed to such things. I had been brought up in a colliery village but this was in a different league. I left Askern that day depressed and wondering what must it be like to live there, not realising that one day in the future, I was destined find out.

Twenty years later fate decreed that I was to work in Askern again, this time as a teacher and soon afterwards to meet and marry Janice, who was born in a house on Avenue Road, a stone's throw away from the coking plant. Not only that, Janice's dad, Bill had worked at the Coalite plant.

One winter day in December some years before I met Janice, I remember walking over the infamous "Coalite Bridge." Again it was cold, wet and miserable and I reflected how little things had changed since that day with the ice cream van. The bridge rose in an elevated position right over the corner of the plant itself, close to the flames, smoke and especially the smell. There were children playing close by and I wondered how it was that such youngsters were not terrified. They had, of course, seen it all before for some of them lived in homes that were only yards away from the coking plant.

As I gazed down into a pool of bright yellow water I remember pondering on the words of a comedian of that time. He had managed to upset the locals of a nearby town by claiming that it was the only place he had visited where the sparrows flew backwards so that they did not get soot in their eyes. I wondered with some amusement to myself what he might have said about Askern, and whether it would have involved jokes about birdsong and sparrows coughing.

After Coalite closed, my wife Janice and I moved to live in Askern and I was soon to escape from teaching. Eventually I was to find myself employed by the community, trying to sort out the legacy of a post-industrial Askern. Often I would walk around that same lake which had so attracted me as a child. Soon I noticed that on certain days there was a bad smell around the lake beside the café. It was a strong sulphurous odour reminiscent of the Coalite Plant and I thought it might be the drains. Not long afterwards I was to learn the history of Askern Spa and how it had always had a sulphurous smell, long before Coalite came on to the scene.

Prior to the opening of the colliery in 1911, Askern had developed as a Victorian spa, rivalling nearby Harrogate and attracting visitors on direct daily trains from as far away as Liverpool. These trains stopped at Manchester (Victoria) with timed connections to Accrington, Blackburn, Rochdale, Bolton, Preston, Blackpool (Talbot Road), Wigan, Southport (Chapel Street) and also Wakefield (Kirkgate), which in turn connected to Dewsbury, Bradford, Brighouse, Huddersfield, Halifax, Todmorden and Burnley. The Harwich Boat Train used to stop twice daily in Askern, giving easy access to and from Europe for those who could afford it. All of this is amazing today, when 'progress' dictates that we no longer even have a railway station in Askern.

The lake is one of the most remarkable and attractive features of Askern and apparently has been around for rather a long time, to say the least, since divers recently recovered a Roman coin from its depths. It was known in Victorian times as The Pool, and it played an important part in the development of the

Askern Lake c. 1890s.

Askern Lake today.

spa. It was described in a guidebook of the time as "giving to the whole village a seaside appeal." The guidebook stated that it was fed by several springs of both fresh and sulphur water and contained "profound pits, the depth whereof was not known." Dr. A. B. Granville, in his 1841 book *The Spas of England – Northern Spas* refers to the Askern waters as so strongly emitting a sulphurous odour that another physician, named Dr Edward Chorley, wrote the following epigram:

> *The devil when passing Askeron*
> *Was asked what he thought thereon:*
> *Quoth Satan -'Judging from the stink.*
> *I can't be far from home, I think'.*

So that was the answer to the smell at the back of the lake; it wasn't the drains after all! The "profound pits" are still there and from them still emanates "the stink." The spa sulphur water from beside the Pool was green in colour, and rather unpalatable to drink. It

was usually warmed for bathing in, but also drunk cold "with rhubarb and magnesia". Fortunately, not all the water was like this, and there were some wells and springs which produced some very pure and palatable water.

The waters of Askern had been mentioned as early as 1734 by a Dr. Short of Sheffield in his book *Mineral Waters of Yorkshire*, but the 1820s saw the real development of its potential. In total, five wells offered visitors curing properties, including the Manor Bath Wells, Terrace Bath Wells, Charity Bath Wells, South Parade Baths, Madder Close Well and the Spa Hydropathic Establishment. A guidebook for visitors boasted of the beautiful scenery and the dry, bracing air. Carriage rides were popular around the local villages and there was a "Lovers' Walk" at the back of the Pool. There were six hotels, and over forty boarding houses in Askern had a room which they let out in the season. It was said that the population of Askern used to treble on a Bank Holiday.

The largest bathhouse was the Spa Hydropathic Establishment. It was situated on grounds overlooking the lake by the side of what is now the A19 trunk road, on land which is presently occupied by our new community building (Alexander House). An article written at the time said that it "commands a magnificent view of the surrounding country...the buildings, standing in three acres of well laid grounds, contained dancing, recreation, dining, drawing, billiard, smoking, reading and writing rooms, and a spacious corridor affords a splendid promenade in winter or unfavourable weather. The whole establishment is well equipped, and affords sitz, douche, shower, needle, Russian and sulphur baths." In total there were over ninety rooms, and the staff included a resident physician and a lady entertainer.

Long before the rise of Harrogate, the waters of the springs found in Askern were reputed to be greatly beneficial in the curing of rheumatism, gout, indigestion and various skin complaints. People travelled considerable distances to visit the spa or "place of healing waters". All this was to change however, when the coal deposits which were being mined around Doncaster and Pontefract were traced to Askern. In 1911, a shaft was sunk and a colliery was opened. The wells were filled in and the "unequalled climate and the best sulphur springs in England" were said to be lost to posterity forever.

A local newspaper dated 20 September, 1912 reported that: "The site chosen for sinking came as a shock to the Askern villagers, for instead of being somewhere on the levels between Askern and Moss, the head works were set up by the picturesque road to Campsall, right on the border of the spa itself, and within a stone's throw of the Hydro and the famous pool." It went on to report "Powerful pumping plant was installed...So successful were the pumping operations, indeed, that for a considerable time Askern Pool was practically drained dry, the water supply of the village was curtailed, and – most serious

Manor Baths c. 1890s.

The Spa Hydropathic c. 1890s.

effect of all – the subsoil in some parts of the village underwent so much subsidence that house walls and ceilings were cracked and some of the buildings, visibly out of the perpendicular, had to be supported by huge timber struts."

However, the water had not disappeared, it is still there below ground where it has run for many thousands or perhaps millions of years. It was tested eight years ago at several sites by a firm of consultants engaged by Askern Town Council, and was found to be as good as it ever was.

Some people are even talking about trying to tap into one of the more palatable springs of mineral water and to bottle it for commercial sale. This is to the great amusement of some of the locals who, knowing much about the recent history of Askern, have suggested that we market the new mineral water as "Coke-a-Coalite." The waters of Askern could now

Building Askern Pit.

The Instoneville pit wheel is a monument to a past way of life.

rise again and who knows – one day we may even reopen the spa.

History in this case has been kind to us, for it has provided us with a potential way forward in the future, and we hope something similar will happen with Sutton Common. Despite the fact that the town has no railway station and an inadequate bus service, Doncaster Metropolitan Borough Council planners in the last Doncaster Unitary Development Plan designated Askern as a "dormitory" or "travel to work" area. This has implications in what we can or cannot do to regenerate our area, because most of it is now designated as "green belt." There are very few places left where any type of industrial development could be sited, even if businesses were queuing up to come into Askern.

Askern has had more that its fair share of industrial grime of late, but all of its industrial scars are now in the process of being healed. The pit and Coalite site is now a country park and there are crops growing on the pit spoil tip. In reality, not many people today

would welcome a lot of new industrial development coming into the town. Major industrial estates are being developed at Adwick and Carcroft, which are only two or three miles down the road. Askern is essentially an attractive 32-square-mile rural ward, and it was to that aspect which we turned to seek our future. Leisure and tourism became the main theme of our Community Action Plan and we looked into our past to see if there was anything that we could capitalise on – the rest is history.

It was with some excitement then that members of our Community Partnership embraced Sutton Common with its potential to act as a "hook" and attract both funding and visitors to our area. The whole archaeological project has acted as a focus for many people in our community. Friendships have been formed, and indeed there are those who mourn the fact that there will not be another archaeological dig.

Most of all it has taught us something new about our past and offered us another potential way forward in the future. As with the mineral water bottling plant mentioned earlier, we have managed to secure some £30,000 of Feasibility Study money to explore some ideas for the future of Sutton Common. We are talking to the Carstairs Countryside Trust about a potential legal agreement with the community through the North Doncaster Rural Trust to secure future access should individuals move on.

However excited some of us might be, we all accept the fact that wetland archaeology on its own is not a potential major tourist attraction. From the earliest stages of our relationship with CCT, we have talked about the potential of some form of reconstruction, possibly of one of the fort's gateways. This would act as an excellent marker for the site but, on its own, would present problems of maintenance. It would

Askern from above Sutton Common. The Iron Age enclosures have provided a focus to the heritage of the area.

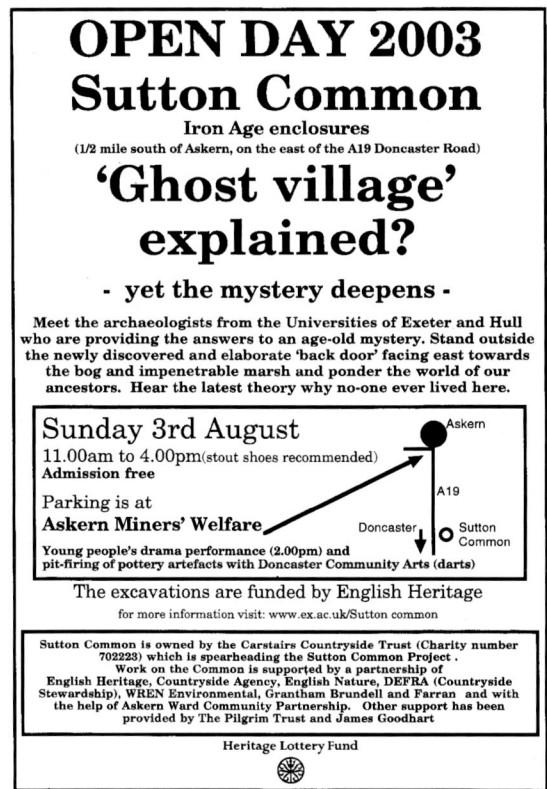

A poster from a Sutton Common Open Day.

also not contribute much to the community and could perhaps act as an attraction for vandals.

We have a great opportunity to do more than this, and a number of options to integrate a range of activities appear to be open to us. However, it is essential that what we do must be financially sustainable in the long term. We know that funders get understandably nervous when people talk to them about sustainable leisure and tourism. This is because of some recent very high profile disasters or near disasters in this field. They include the outrageously-expensive Millennium Dome in London, the ill-fated Popular Music Centre in Sheffield and the local Earth Centre in Mexborough, which recently closed.

Becoming financially sustainable or economically viable is not easy. The way apparently favoured by the Government, through its Regional Development Agency (Yorkshire Forward), is to try to create a commercial business that generates sufficient income to sustain itself. But all new commercial businesses have a high failure rate, and that is especially worrying for community volunteers seeking to attract and invest public money in a way forward.

An alternative way is to provide a service facility which fulfils a community need and try to attract state funding to maintain it. Unfortunately for us, most funding that finds its way into community pockets is short-term. The long-term "core" funding goes into local authorities and statutory services like police, fire, education and health. Most successful community projects try to combine grant funding of some sort with earned income.

Anyone with a little effort can create some income, but generating sufficient regular return to sustain a project which employs a number of staff is a much greater challenge. In order to do so you have to be commercially competitive and mercenary enough to survive in the real world. That often means sacrificing your principles. As a friend of mine often says when I chide him over his business dealings: "It's not robbery Howard – it's business, it's business."

One way forward is to take a historical theme and try to wrap some commercial ideas around it. Leaving the Iron Age aside for one moment, to illustrate what I mean let's have a bit of fun by taking a nearby pub and seeing how we could develop this idea by exploiting its link to a famous person in the past.

The Sun Inn on the nearby Great North Road is a fairly modern building which replaced an old coaching hostelry in which the famous highwayman Dick Turpin is supposed to have lodged as he rode between London and York.

One could easily remodel the place in the manner of "Ye Olde Pub" complete with obligatory beams (plastic) and appropriate artifacts (brass). It could perhaps be renamed "Turpin's Lodge", as there is already a pub named "The Highwayman" two miles down the road. And of course it would sell "Old Ale." Included would be a restaurant, possibly named "The Stables," which would have period lighting (candles) so that you can't see what you are eating. The restaurant would serve an appropriate specialist menu including dishes like "Black Bess Burgers" with horse-radish sauce and "Turpin's Treacle Tart". A childrens' section could be a tidy earner with themed parties and

The Sun Inn.

a sideline in selling hats, masks and plastic guns. Then, of course, you could rob the patrons with the prices you charged in the restaurant and over the bar. Far-fetched? Well, I may have exaggerated and contrived the above example to make it rather more hysterical than historical, but I have certainly been in places that were not too dissimilar. It is not the type of approach we would want to see associated with Sutton Common, even if it did have the potential to be profitable, so let us examine some other potential pathways to sustainability.

An educational institution might attract a stable funding stream from the Government through the Learning and Skills Council. We certainly have a good case for this in Askern, since we are in the top two per cent of most educationally deprived wards in the country. It has been suggested that we build some kind of study centre for children connected with the common. This would exploit the fact that it is an Iron Age Site but it would need a slightly wider focus for, would you believe it, the Iron Age is not in the National Curriculum. Therefore it could perhaps embrace environmental issues. It might or might not have residential facilities and attract children from all over Doncaster and beyond. But on its own, it might have severe limitations.

A more beneficial approach for the local community might be to build a Further or Higher Education Centre. This ties in with the proposed new Doncaster University, which although having a central hub in the town centre is intended to have satellite facilities out in the community. This could be one of the proposed "Gateway" facilities which would retain its independence from the university proper. We could also try to build an Arts Centre or Performance Venue and again, Doncaster College is looking to do something similar as part of the proposed university development.

The disused RAF Finningley aerodrome – now on the threshold of a new era as the Robin Hood Doncaster Sheffield International Airport.

An idea of mine which has caught many people's imagination is also related to a major new development in Doncaster. Work is well advanced on developing the redundant RAF Finningley airfield into the new 'Robin Hood Doncaster Sheffield' airport, which will attract international traffic. A local tourism officer has told me that the developers are looking for ideas for projects which will attract people to Doncaster itself. The fear is that Doncaster will simply be a place that people will just pass through on their journey to other destinations. To a certain extent, that is inevitable, for that is the nature of an airport. However, it would be nice if we had something which attracted people to Doncaster as a destination and encouraged them to spend their money here.

If one is not fixed on the idea that Sutton Common is simply an Iron Age site but acknowledge that it is part of a time line in the history of Askern, or indeed the world, then all sorts of possibilities open up. Each one of us is part of that time line, for we have connections through our ancestors which stretch back to the beginning of time. Each one of us has two parents, whether we knew them both or not, and each of our parents in turn had two parents, for such is the nature of how we reproduce.

The access route between the Sutton Common enclosures and Askern – the horizon would once have been dominated by the mine and Coalite Works.

This means that the number of people that we are descended from doubles with every generation. Everybody understands this; it is not rocket science that we have two parents, four grandparents, and eight great grandparents and so on. However, few stop to think how many people this relates us to in just a couple of hundred years, let alone going back into the far distant past.

In family history terms, a generation is calculated at 30 years because that is the average length of time, evened out over years, for each new generation of children to grow up and start having children of their own. Applying this rule means that a child born today in 2004 will have two parents who on average were born around 1974. That child will in turn will have four grandparents who were born around 1944 and eight great-grandparents who were born around 1914 – the year the First World War broke out. Carrying on back into history, by the time we reach the Battle of Hastings in 1066, a date that most people seem to know, we find that we are related to four billion, two hundred and ninety four million, nine hundred and sixty seven thousand, two hundred and ninety six people (4,294,967,296). It is interesting then that the total population of the earth was estimated to be only around four hundred and fifty million (450,000,000) in the year 1300, which was 234 years later.

The figures start to appear wrong because they imply that the child is related to over nine times the total population of the earth at that time. However, that only holds true if every one of our ancestors was different and we were only related to each of them once. By the time we get so far back, we are talking about relationships rather than individuals. We are in fact related to the same people many times through many different ancestral routes. In other words, the same people appear many times in different places on our ancestral family tree. The fact that everybody's lines start to cross and create such a vast number of overlaps throw up some interesting possibilities.

For example, does that mean that we are all descendents of William the Conqueror? Because of a lack of written records at the time, it is virtually impossible to prove or disprove that fact even through known relationships, although many try. And then, of course, there were the unknown relationships for many early kings were not slow to use, or rather abuse, their positions of power! Even today, confidential surveys in America involving blood tests have shown that as many as 10 per cent of people in the surveys cannot have the father that they think they have. In short, statistics show that it would be highly unlikely if you were *not* related to William the Conqueror – but then proving it is another matter!

Moving back to the Iron Age, which was 1,500 years before William won the Battle of Hastings, we find that we have travelled back 84 generations, and a child born today would have a potential 19,342,813,113,834,100,000,000,000 ancestors. The total population of the world around 600 years later in 100AD has been estimated to be around one hundred and sixty millions (160,000,000). Don't ask me how they calculated it. Even today, the total population of the world was only estimated to pass the six billion (6,000,000,000) mark in 1999. This means that the child's potential ancestral line in the Iron Age is 3,223,802,185,639,017 TIMES the total world population today. It would be 120,892,581,961,463,125 TIMES the total world population in 100AD.

The implications of this are that everybody, certainly in the Western World, is related to somebody on Sutton Common. Why not celebrate this fact by build-

Looking to the future. Stalwart local supporter, Bev Weigel, enjoys a helicopter ride to see the Askern area from the air.

ing a Family History Centre linked to it? Maybe even the National Centre for Family History, perhaps combined with other uses? Family history is apparently the second most popular subject on the World Wide Web – after sex. I know that the above applies to any site of antiquity, but it is our idea and we should perhaps try to capitalise on it.

Such a centre would have the potential to draw in international visitors through Finningley from all over the world, as well as visitors from all over Britain. It could to be a "One Stop Shop" for both family and local history, since the two are closely linked. It would need to contain research rooms with major Internet links, a library, a shop, a conference venue with lecture facilities, a restaurant or café and adequate parking. It would have to be a repository for local archives and have links to all kinds of institutions and organisations from Civil Registration to the Mormons in Salt Lake City. It could arrange package deals for transport and accommodation.

From above the Miners' Welfare looking toward Sutton Common and the disused Thorpe Marsh power station beyond.

People could even get married there, perhaps in a reconstruction of the site. Iron Age Weddings? Is that a step too far? Is it starting to sound like the pub idea again, or the marriage chapels in Las Vegas? The possibilities are limited only by the co-operation and support we can enlist, the funding we can obtain, the financial viability of such a project and not least by the effort that we are prepared to put into it. One way or another, the soon-to-be commissioned Feasibility Study should give us some answers.

Oh yes, and before I forget, that number again. I am sure you would like to know how to read it. So here goes:- nineteen septillions, three hundred and forty two sextillions, eight hundred and thirteen quintillions, one hundred and thirteen quadrillions, eight hundred and thirty four trillions and one hundred billions... That should win you a few pints in the pub, but please – not in Turpin's Lodge!

HOWARD CONNELL

Howard, the project manager for the North Doncaster Rural Trust, was born in Doncaster and brought up in nearby Woodlands. He attended the Percy Jackson Grammar School, Doncaster College of Art and Sunderland College of Education, where he specialised in Art (Ceramics) and Music. Howard taught in first and middle schools for 25 years and held positions of responsibility for Arts, Crafts and Music. He was a founder member of Adwick Amateur Swimming Club and Doncaster Society for Family History.

CONCLUSION

THE MARCH OF TIME

Time Present and Time past, are both perhaps present in time future,
and time future contained in time past

(T.S.Eliot)

Wednesday, 27 July 2003, 10.00 am. Askern Miners' Welfare Club. Time Present and Time Past – a conference to celebrate a truly joined-up-job.

Monday, 24 November 2003, 5.00 pm. Houlsby Centre, Sutton Road, Askern. CCT meet North Doncaster Rural Trust to chart the next steps.

Tuesday, 2 December 2003, 2.15 pm. Houlsby Centre. The Sutton Common Group reflect on seven year's work and choose this as the moment in 'the march of time' to tell the story and write this book.

Unravelling the distant past is like looking into a marshy pool; predicting the future, akin to gazing into a crystal ball. Both need vision to create a picture. Both, looked at from the present, are incomplete. We cannot alter the past, only understand it better. But we can at least dream about the future, knowing the only limits to achievement are our energy and imagination.

Will we find out one day what Sutton Common was all about? Yes, I think we will; those posts heading towards the bog and new circular crop marks recently spotted from his tractor by Andrew Booth, both might have stories to tell. What about restoring the fortunes of this community? Yes, it will put itself firmly on the map – it is already on its way. And, yes, the Sutton Common Project, perhaps one day with a fine reconstruction of the gateways, will play a part; those curious, inconspicuous humps on the Common a testimony that from seemingly so little, an enormous amount can grow.

Our vision for the Common *will* become a reality, as visitors find out, learn, think and imagine what it must have been like here long ago.

Why am I so hopeful? Because we have already come a great distance… and all through a simple vision, a map, a great deal of trust and a lot of goodwill.

But people and time move on. We are just a part of the ever-changing story, shaping, deciding, investigating, building, promoting, convincing … but most of all enjoying an amazing experience. We are living out a little collective dream, I suppose.

Time *has* marched on, and we *have* indeed all come a very long way since Jon Etté told his sad tale in the pub, and since June, Peter and their parish council welcomed us in. We hope they are pleased with what they see.

Ian Carstairs

Andrew Booth, farmer, his foot on a root of prehistoric bog oak, with Joy Allan, Chairman of the Carstairs Countryside Trust, under a pylon built on one of the Mesolithic island sites at Sutton Common.

PHOTOGRAPHIC CREDITS

APS (UK) – Beverley: 8, 10, 28, 30, 36, 53, 65, 86 left, 96, 97, 103, 110, 113, 116.

Ian Carstairs: 9, 14, 16, 17, 19 top, 20, 21, 22, 25, 27, 29, 32, 39, 41, 42, 45, 52, 54 left, 69, 82, 86 right, 87, 88, 90, 91, 92 left, 94 left, 95 right, 98, 99 top,100, 101, 118, back cover.

Doncaster Museums and Archives Service, Doncaster Metropolitan Borough Council: 11 (Peter Snowball), 34, 37, 38 left.

Herbert Ballard – Hull: 12 ,47, 72.

Barbara Riddle: 19.

English Heritage, National Monuments Records (D. Riley collection) – Swindon: 40.

Universities of Exeter and Hull, Sutton Common Project: 54, 55, 56, 57, 59, 60, 62, 63, 64, 92 right.

Joy Allan: 58.

Andrew Booth: 66, 94 right, 95 left; 99 bottom, 114.

James Cheetham: 73, 77.

David Patrick: 83, 84.

Howard Connell: 106 right, 112, 115.